Sit the F*CK down and color

SWEAR WORD ADULT COLORING BOOK

31 ILLUSTRATIONS USING THE WORD F*CK

Life is full of things that stress us out. Between work, children, bills, and chores at home, our minds are inundated with stuff vying for our attention. Coloring is a great way to relax and allow stress to melt away.

Have a problem you are trying to figure out? Just open up this book, take your colored pencils, and begin filling in the blank spaces. Don't focus on anything, but coloring what is within this book. By doing this, you will clear you mind, and just might come up with the solution you've been searching for.

With 31 designs, all featuring the word fuck, to color, this book has something for every skill level. So just take a moment, relax, and color.

You can tear this page out and use it to put between the images so as to avoid bleed through.

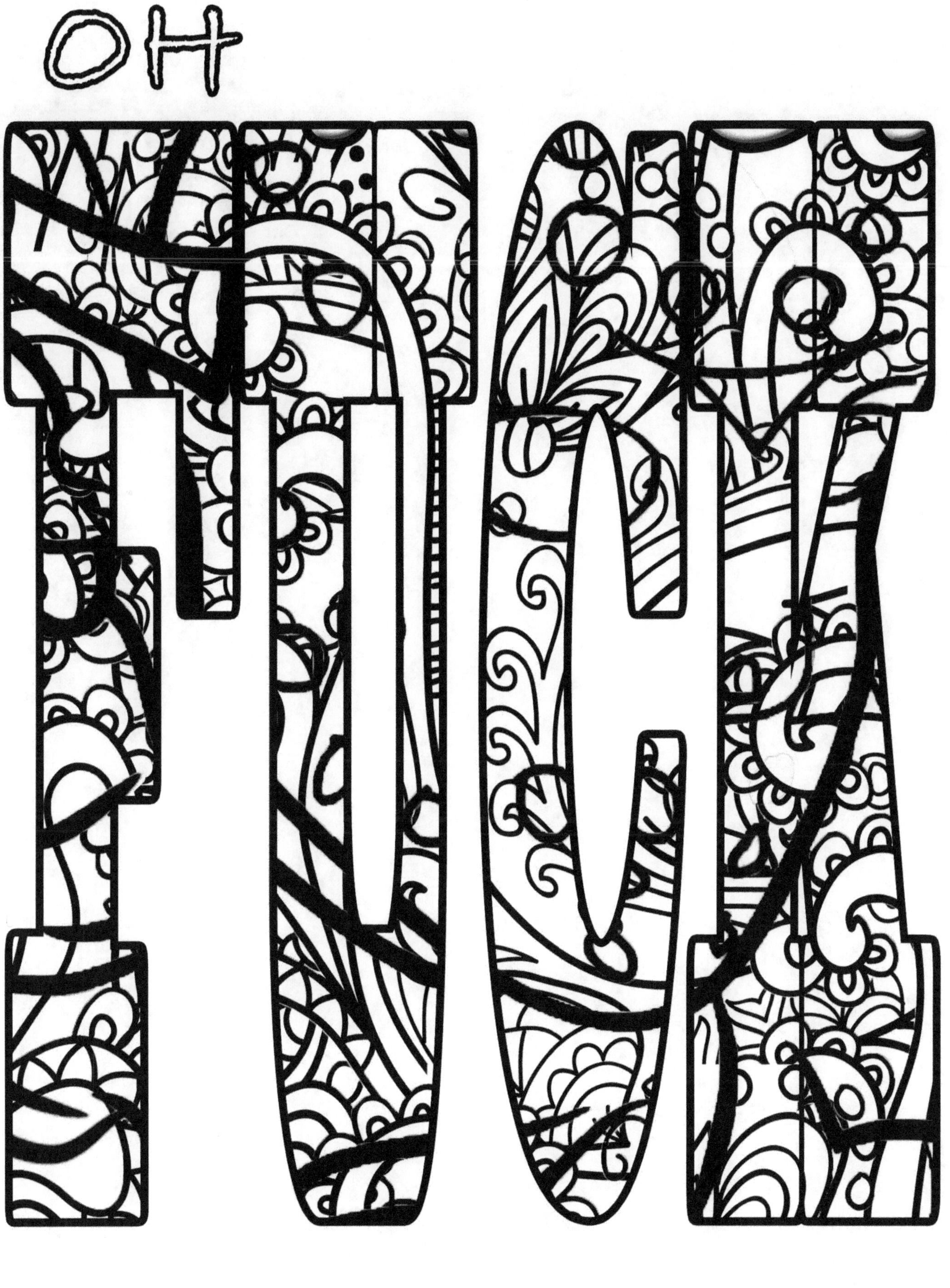
OH
FUCK

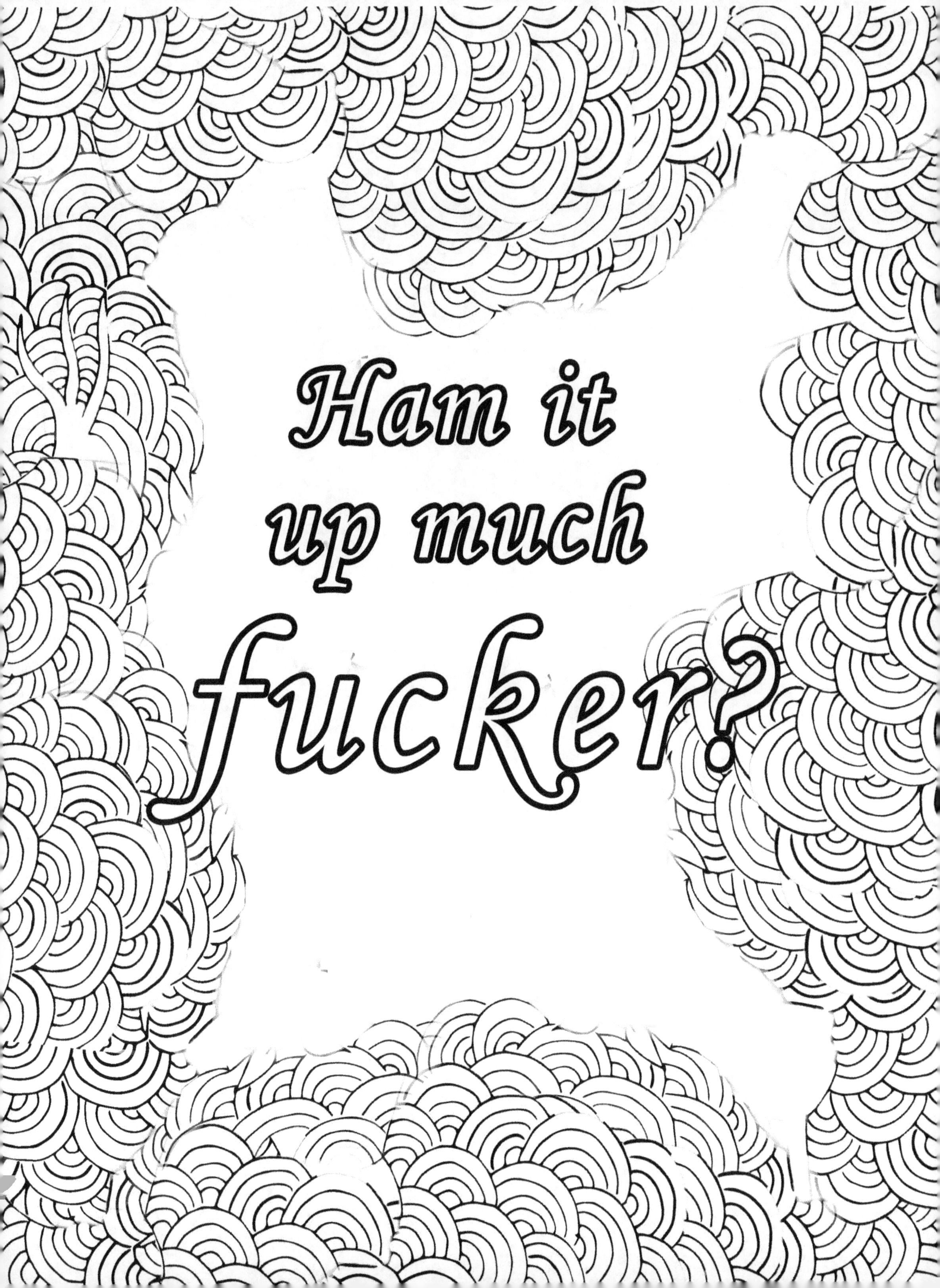
Ham it
up much
fucker?

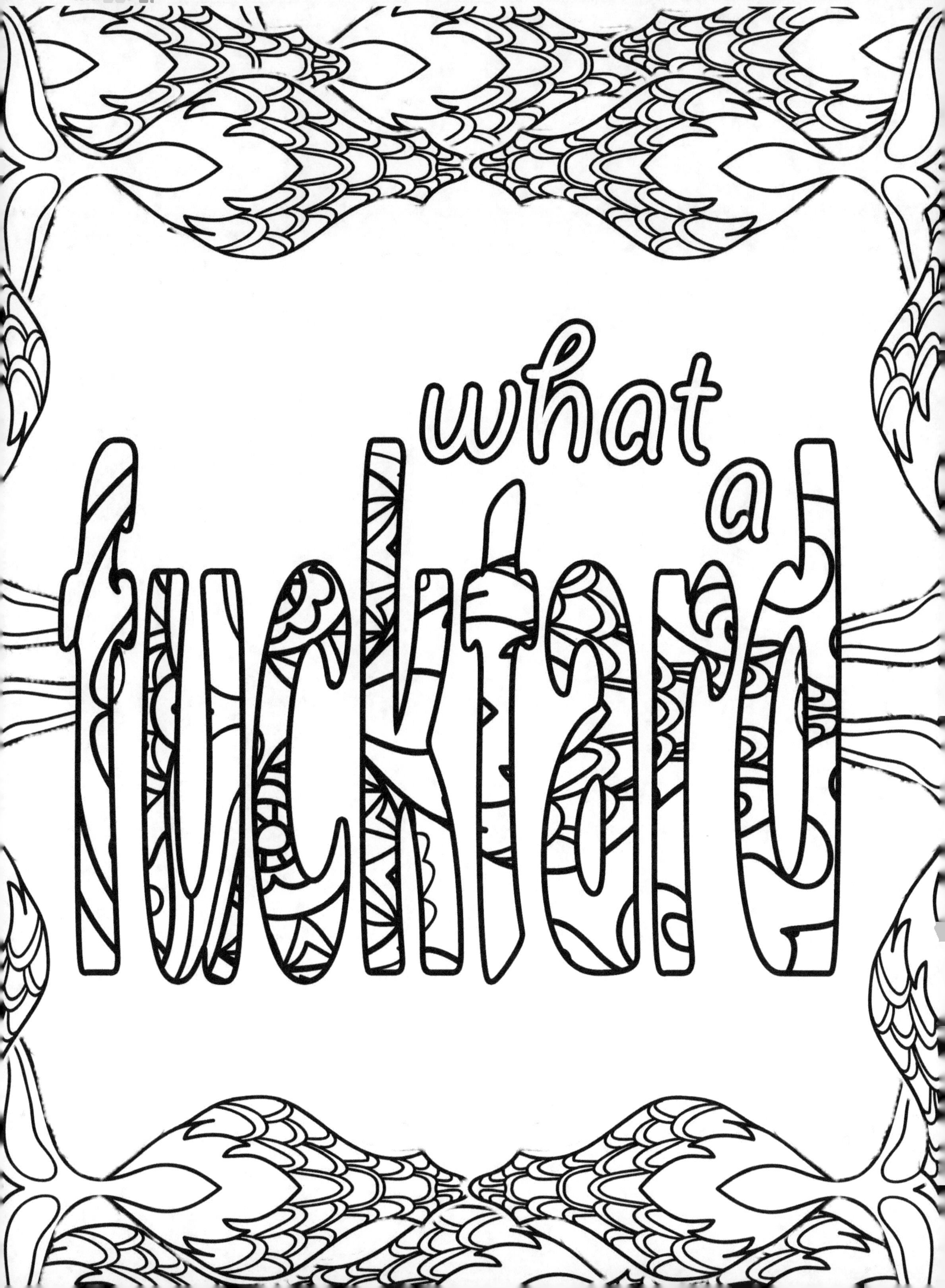
what a
fucktard

IF I WANTED YOUR OPINION, I'D ASK FOR IT. SO....

FUCK OFF!

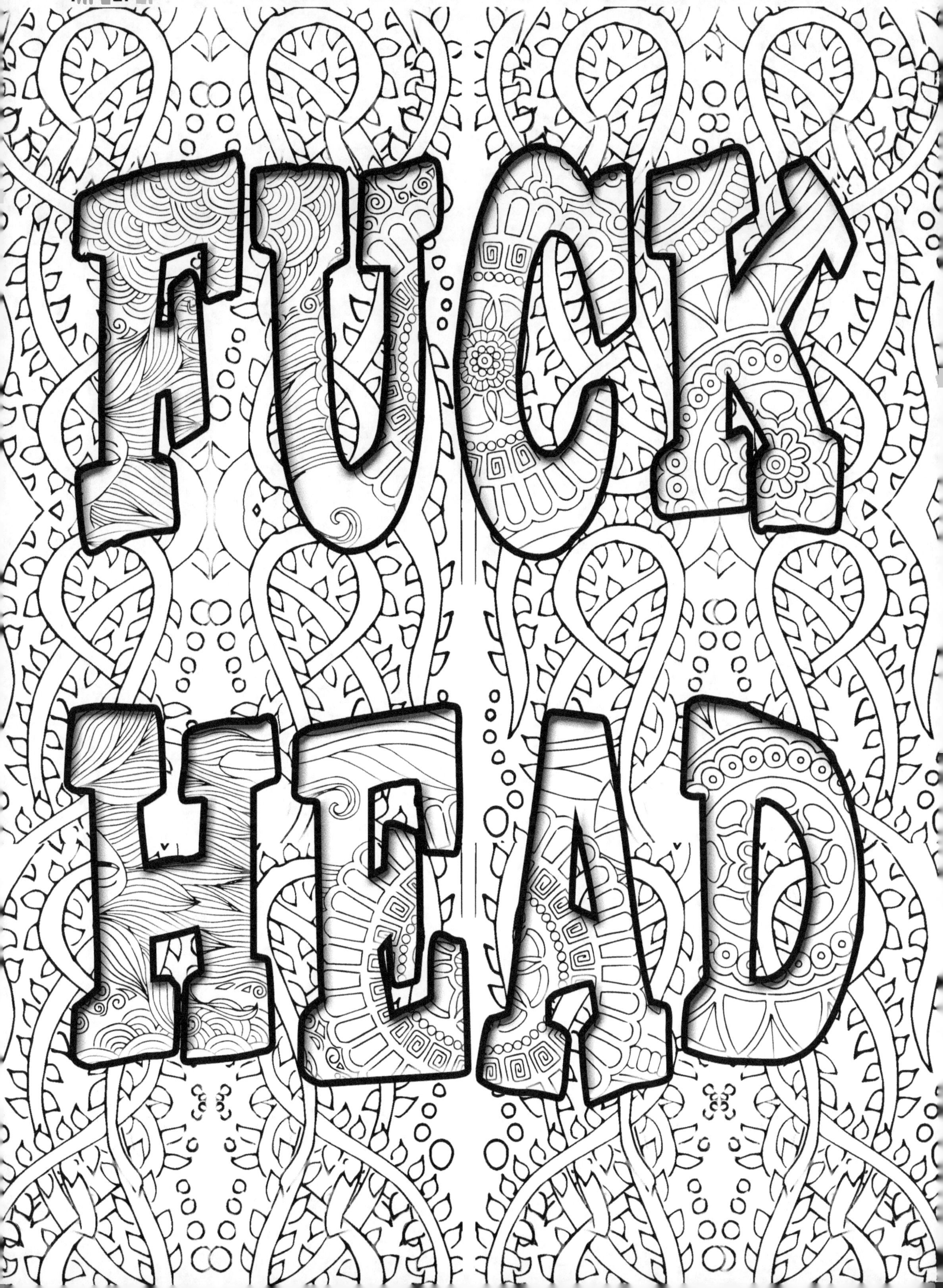
FUCK
HEAD

It’s not a
brain fart;
it’s a
brain fuck.

FUCK TART

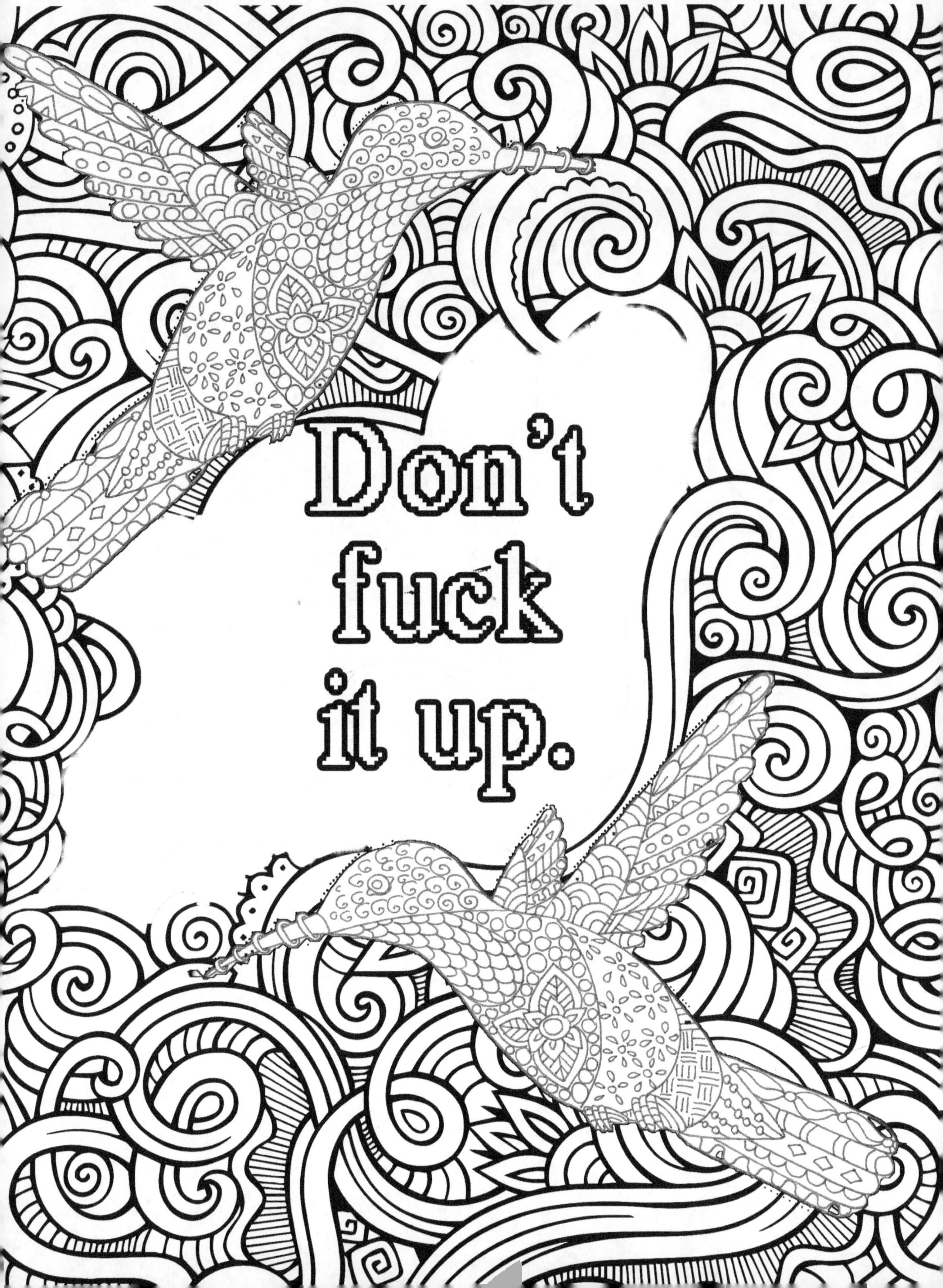
Don't fuck it up.

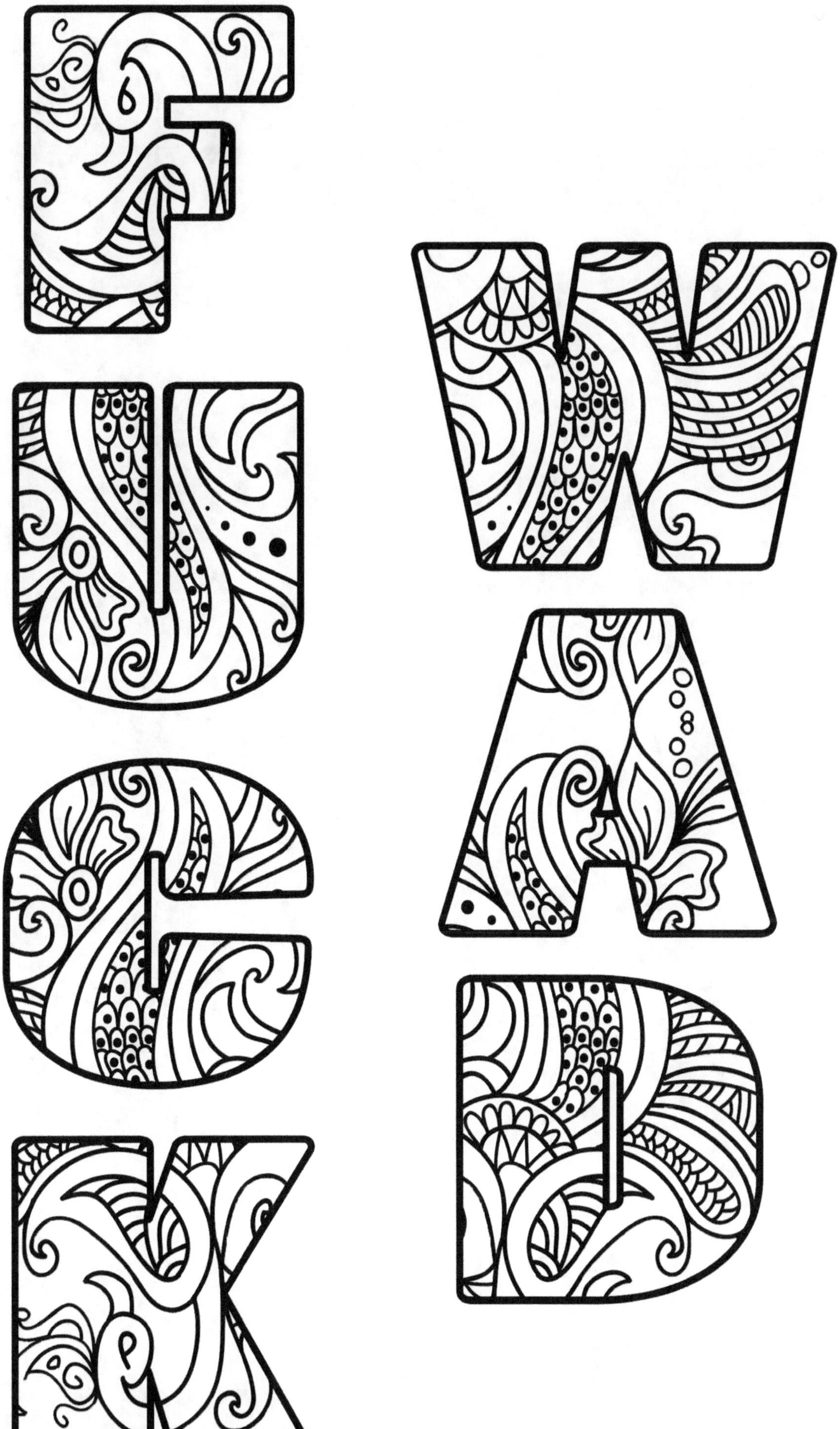
FUCK
WAD

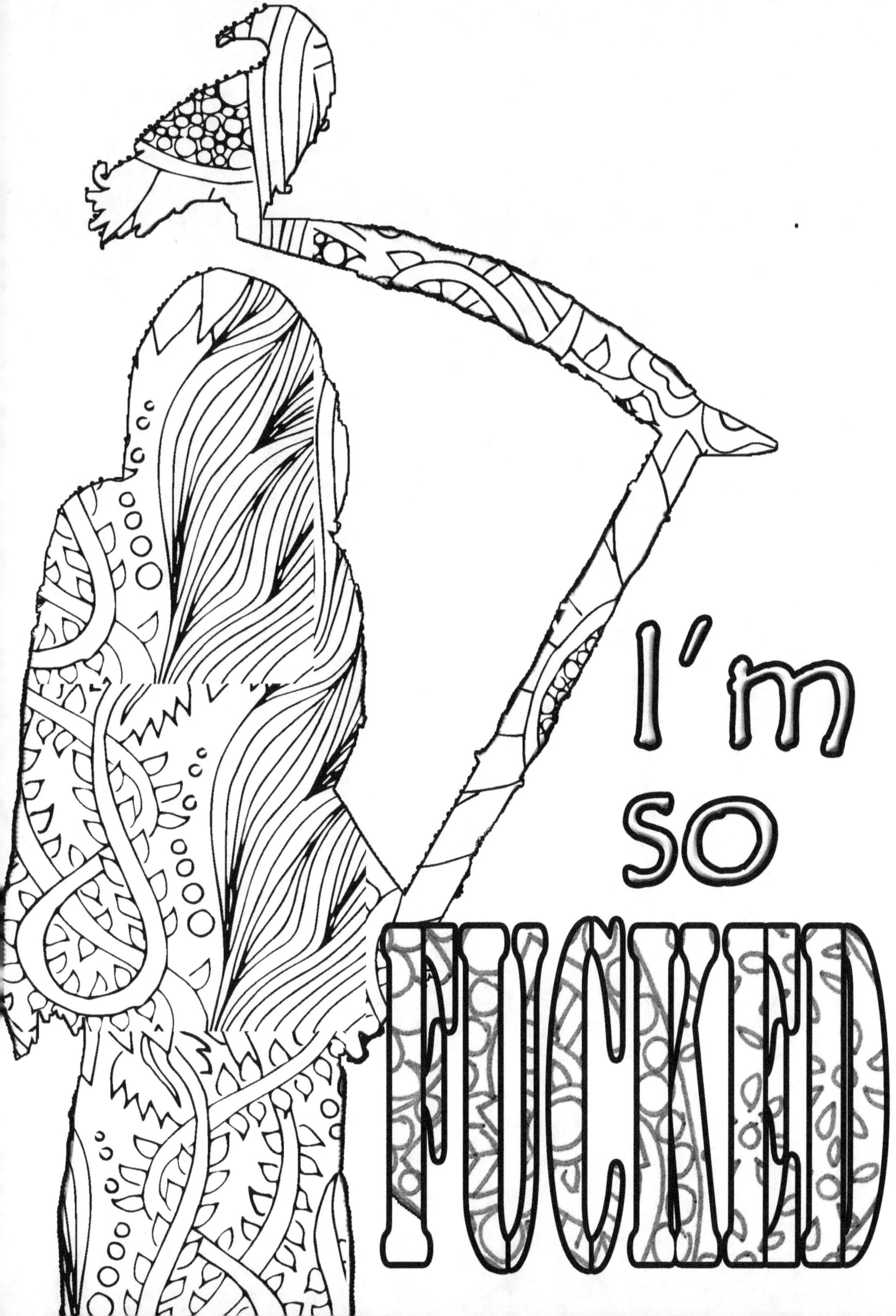
I'm so
FUCKED

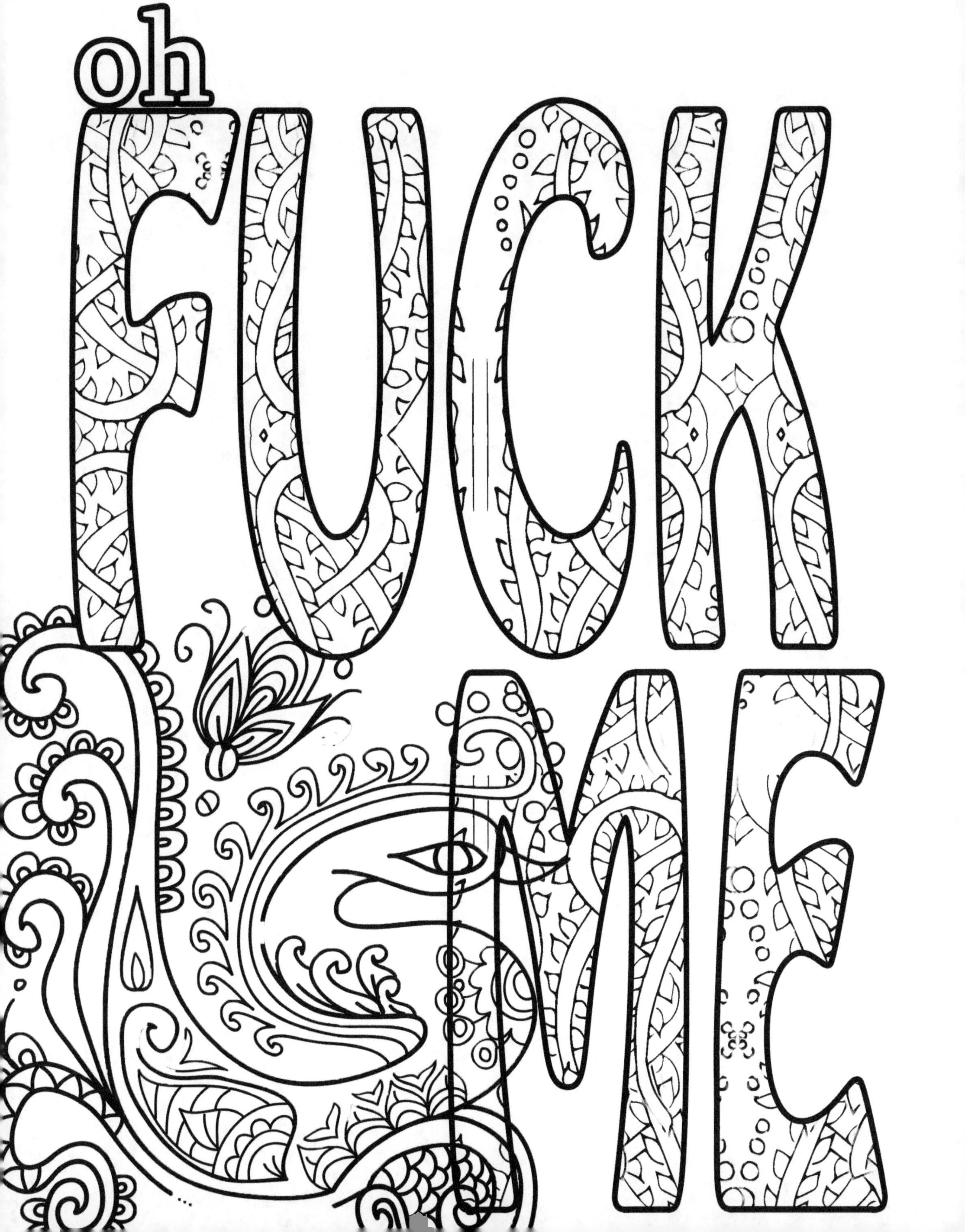
oh
FUCK
ME

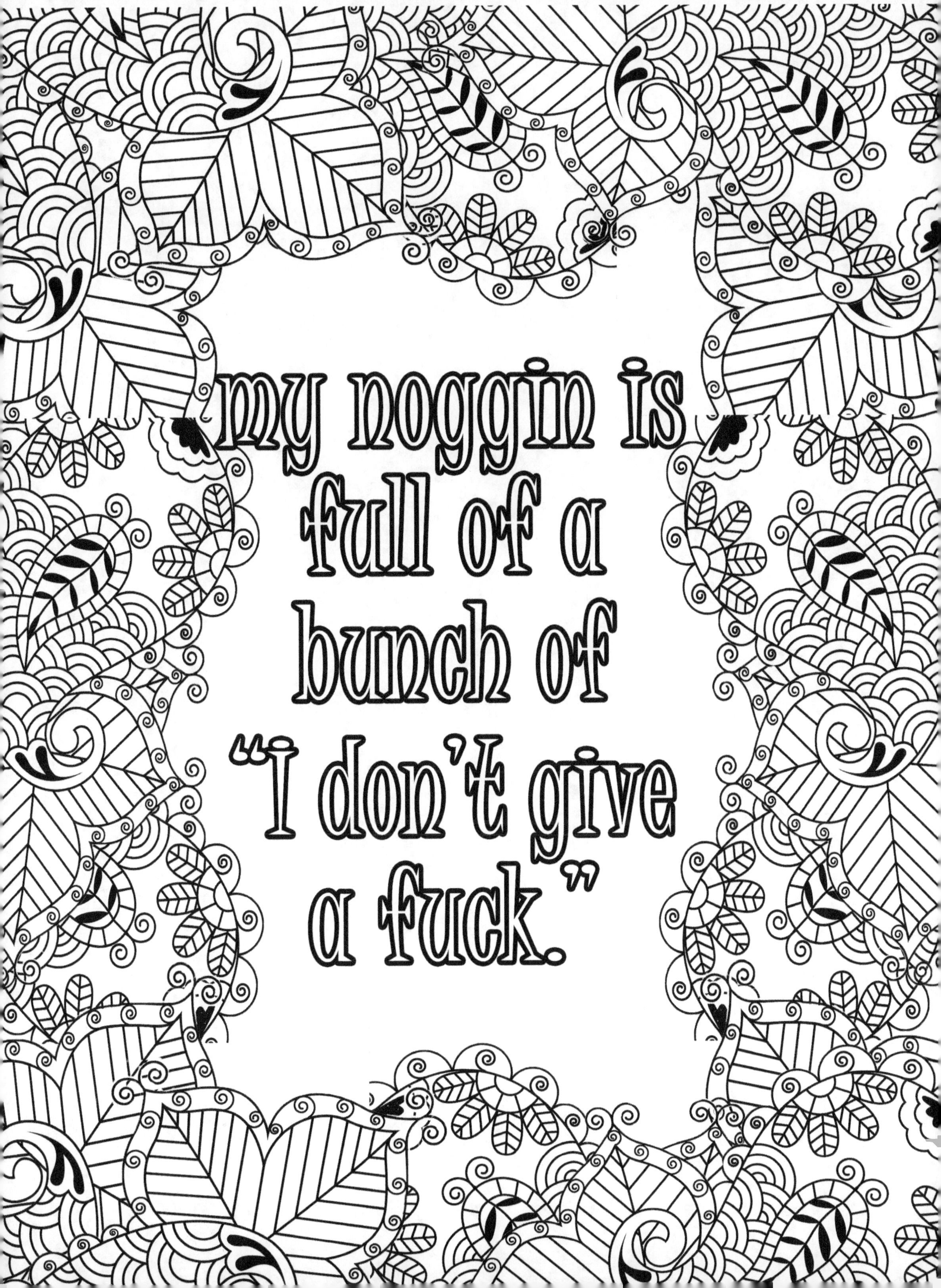
my noggin is
full of a
bunch of
"I don't give
a fuck."

My squirrel says you are a

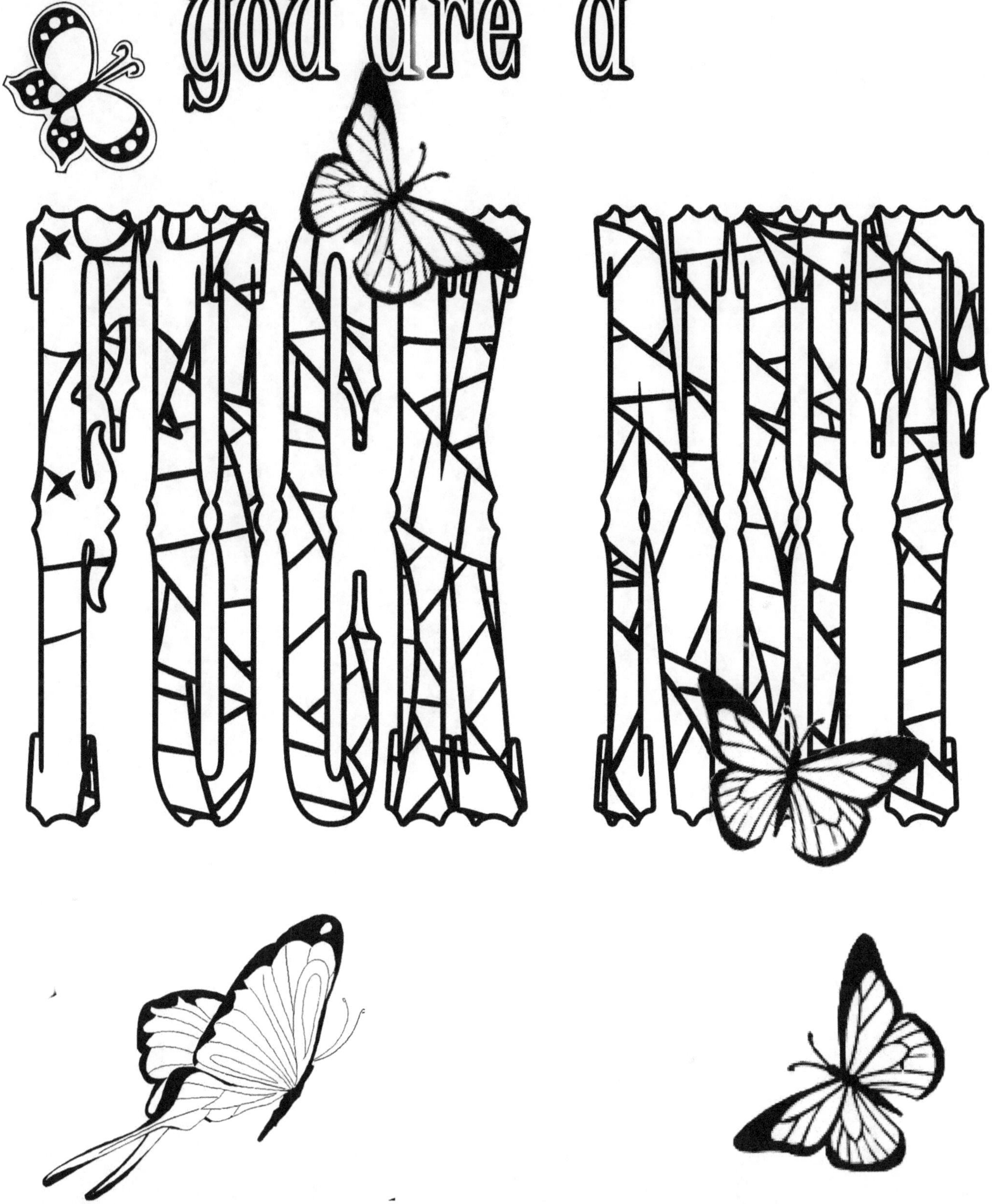

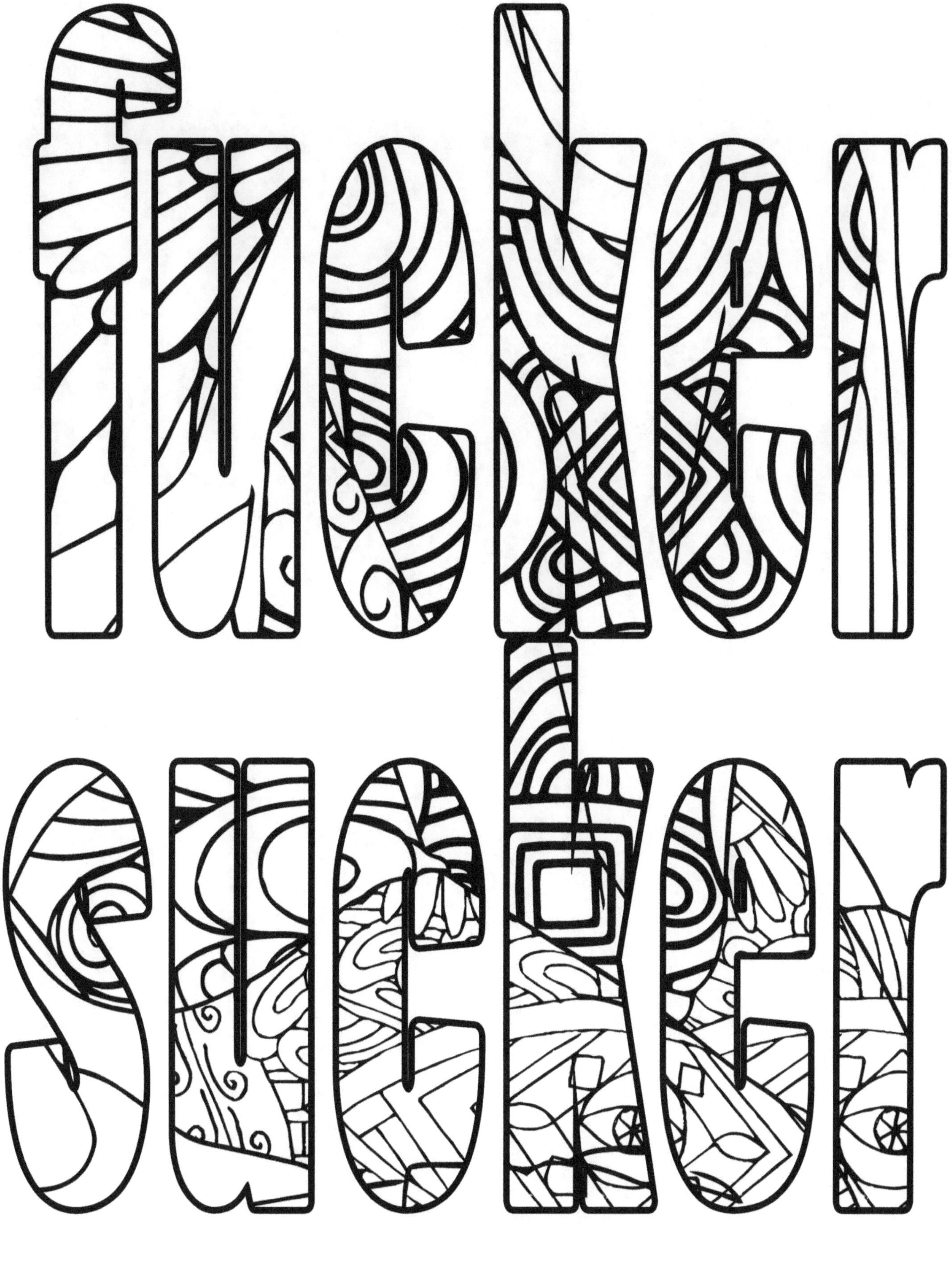
fucker
sucker

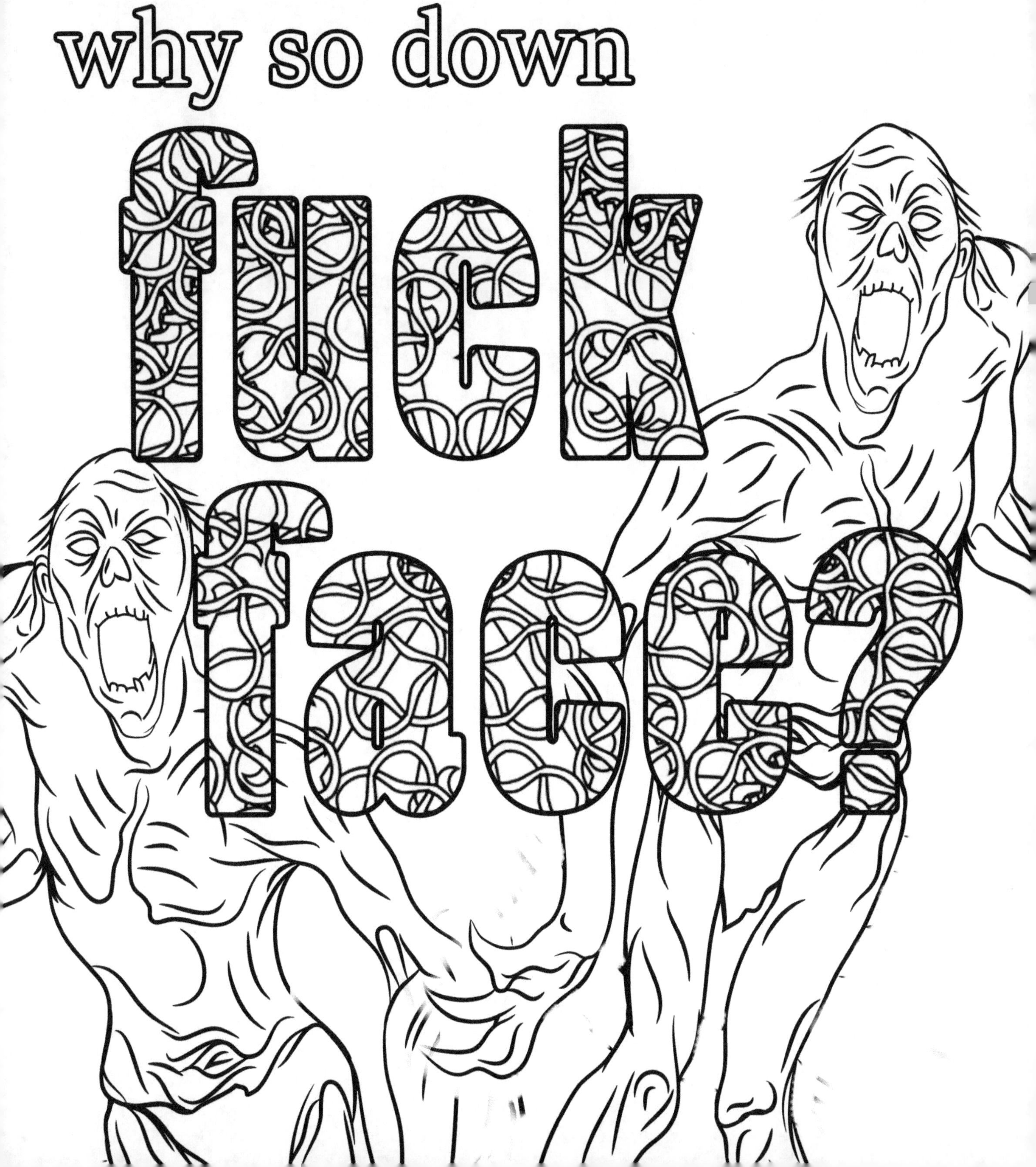
why so down
fuck
face?

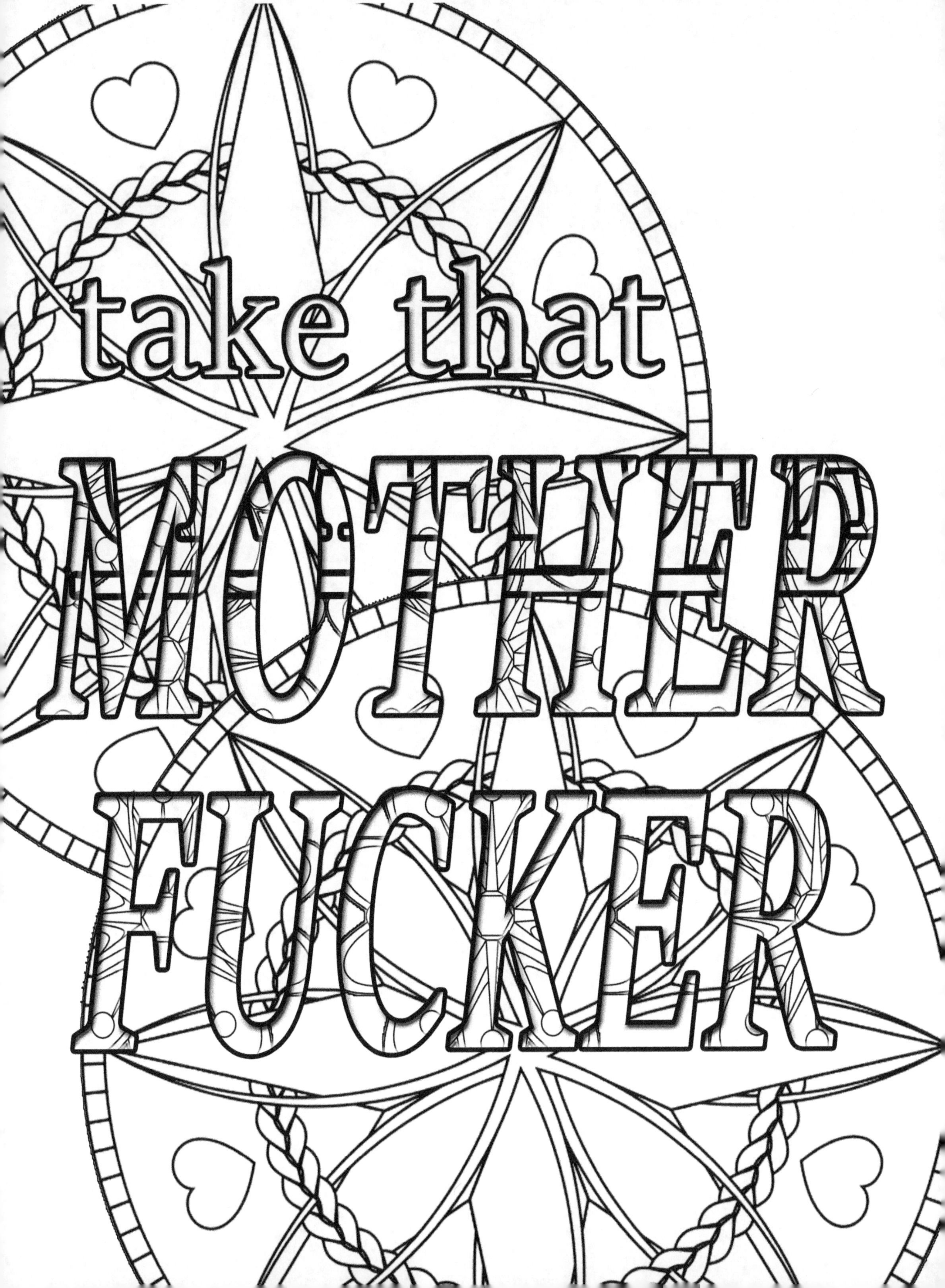
take that
MOTHER
FUCKER

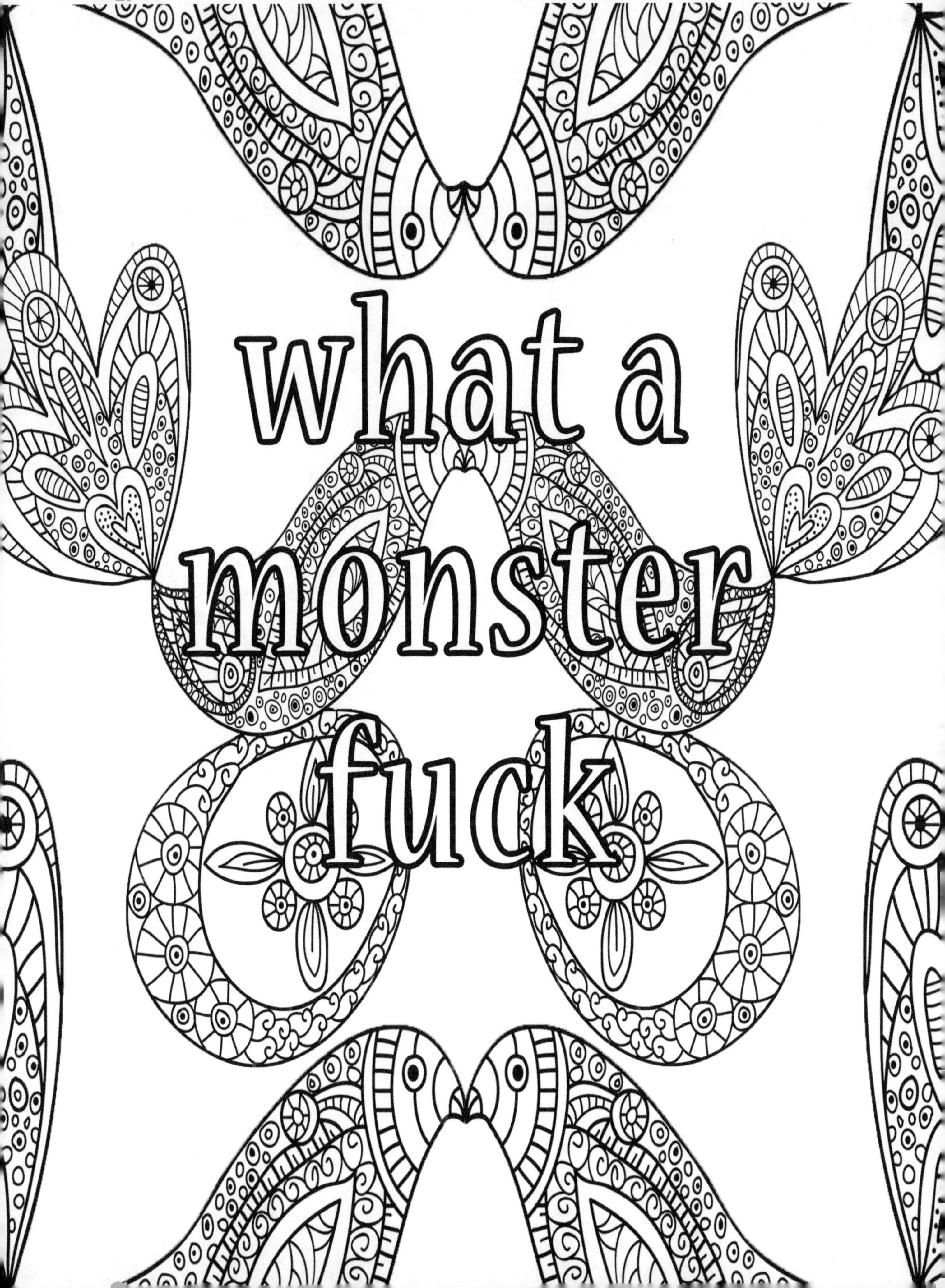
what a
monster
fuck

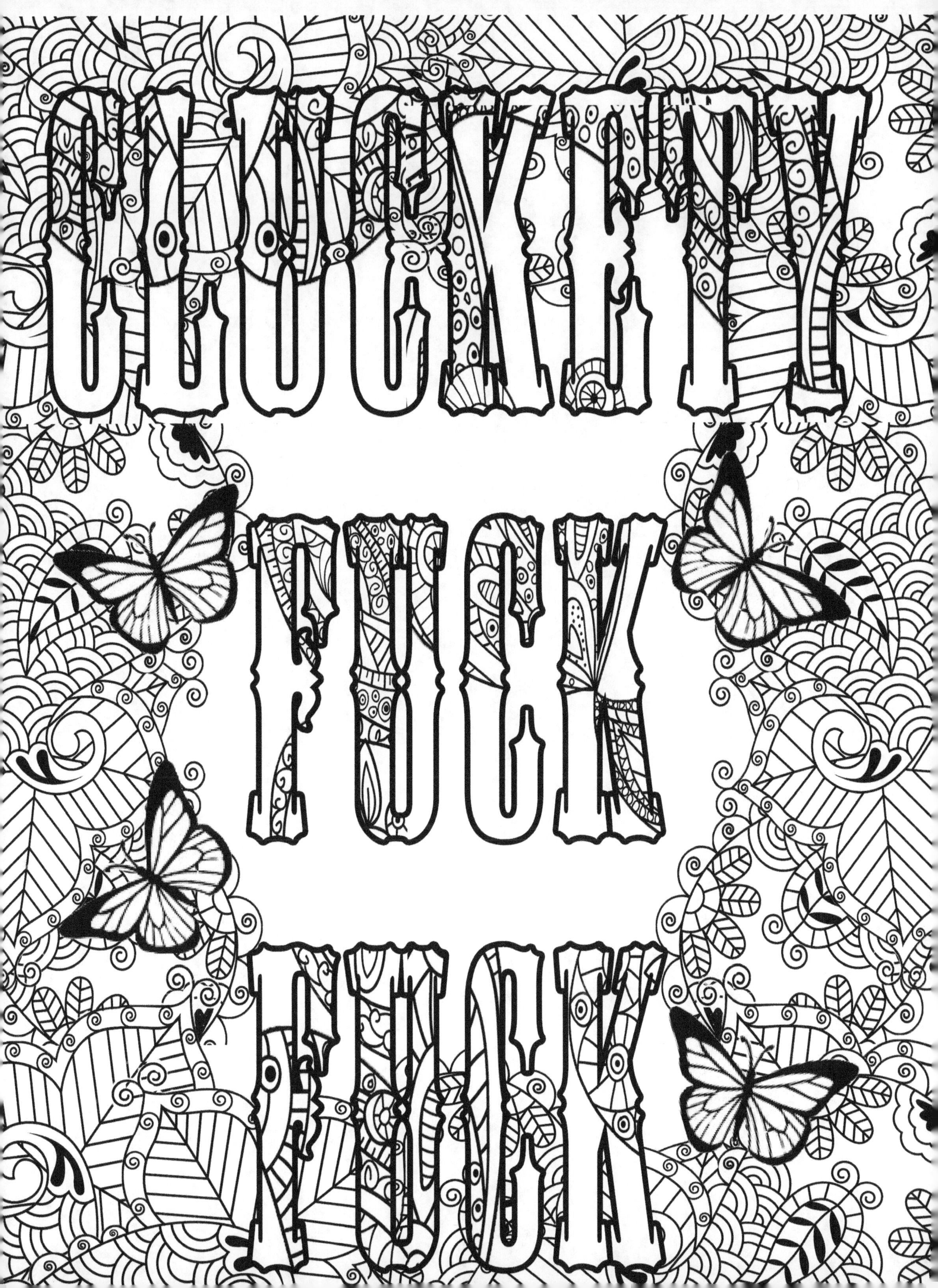
CLUCKETY
FUCK
FUCK

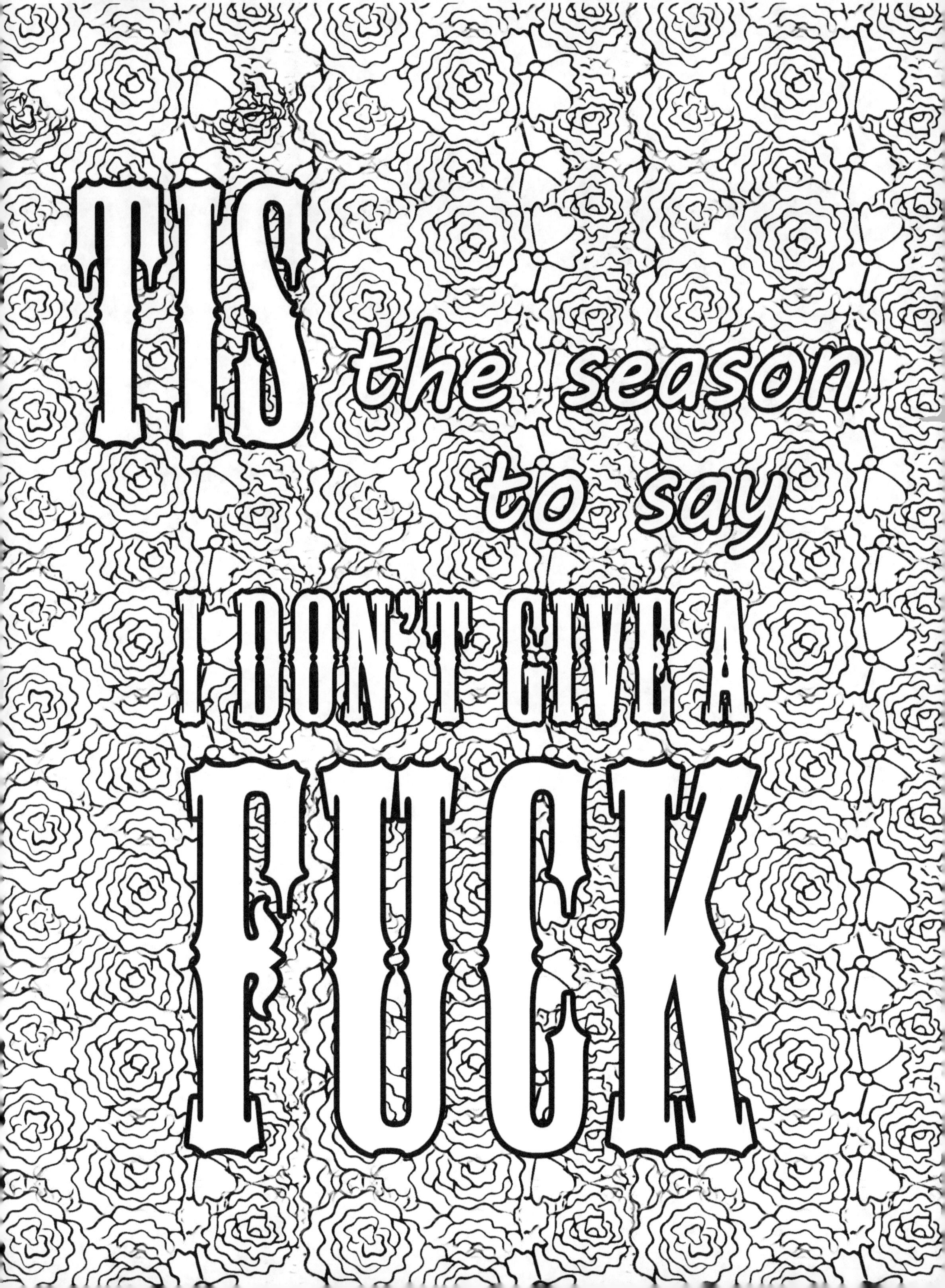
TIS the season
to say
I DON'T GIVE A
FUCK

My quota of

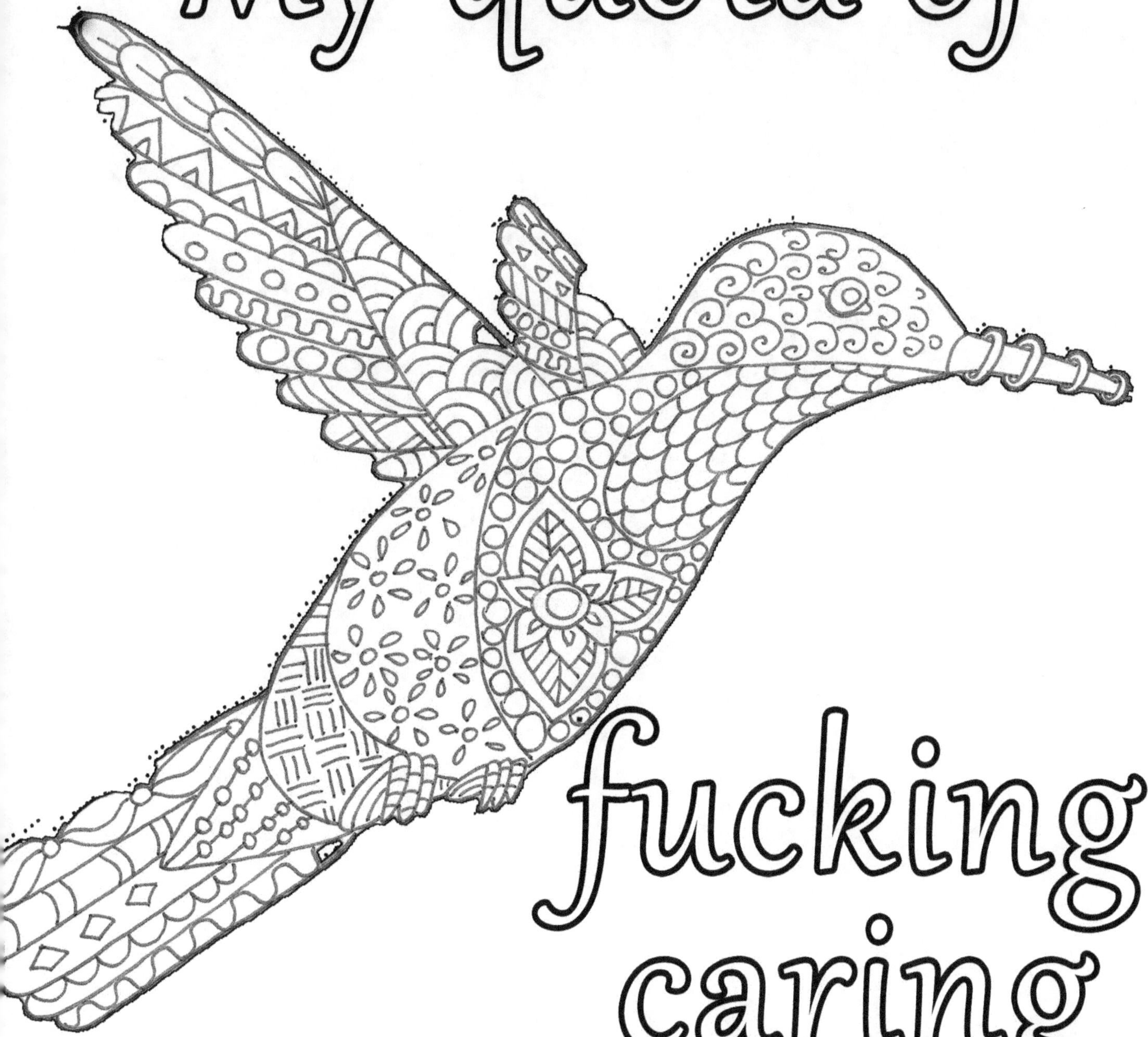

fucking
caring
was exceeded
years ago.

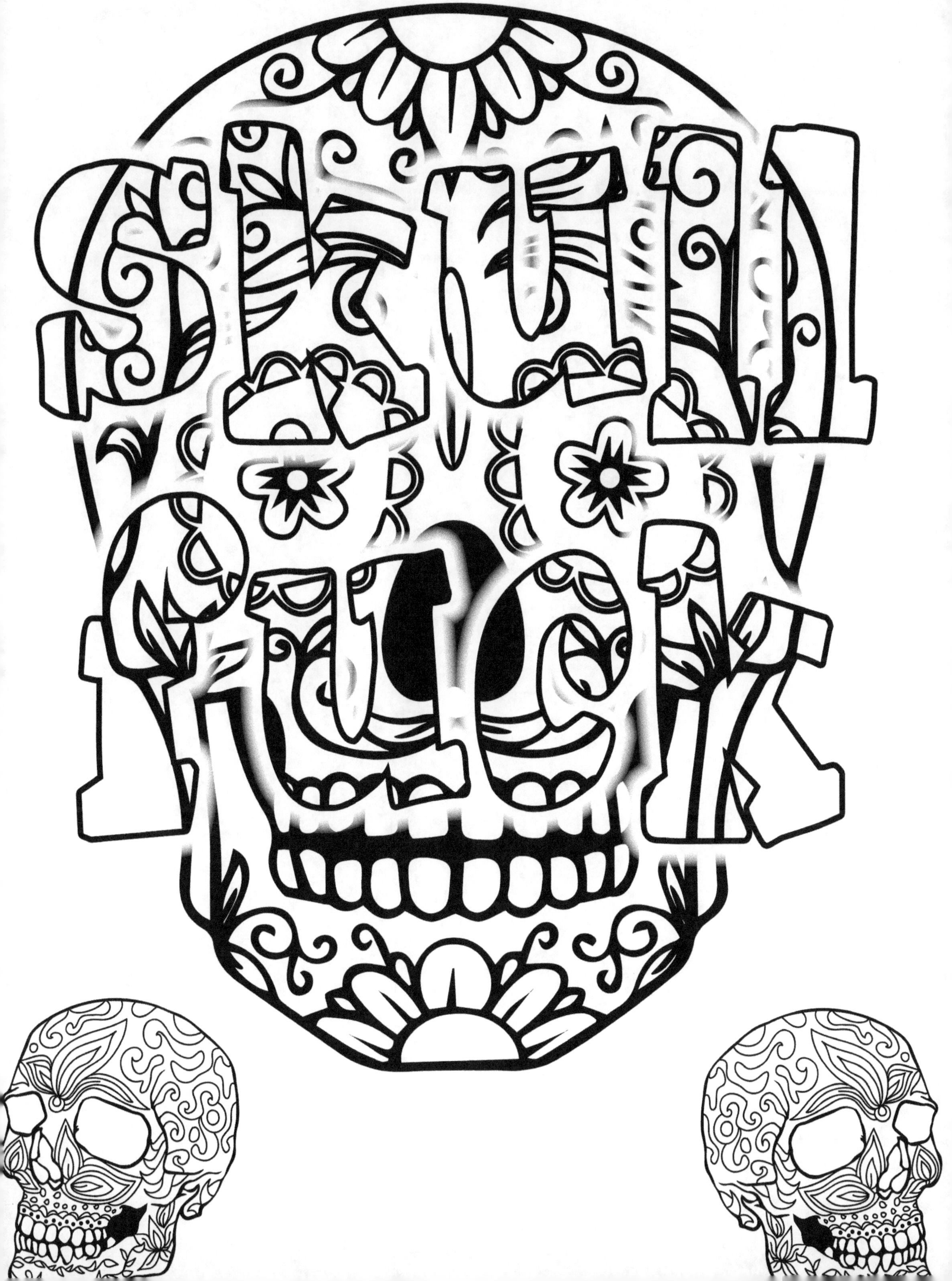
Skull Rock

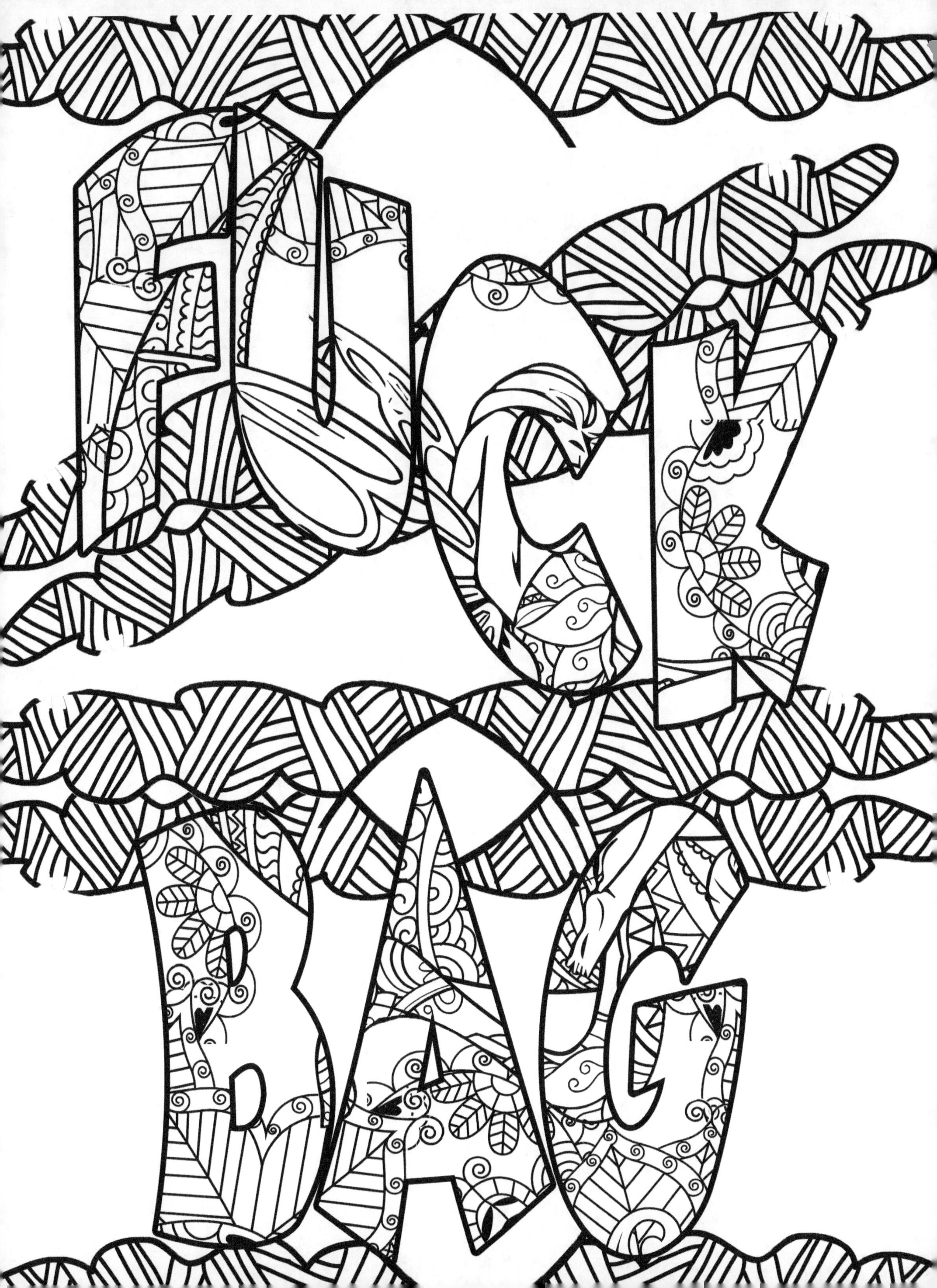
FUCK
BAG

What's on your mind
FUCK
BUTT?

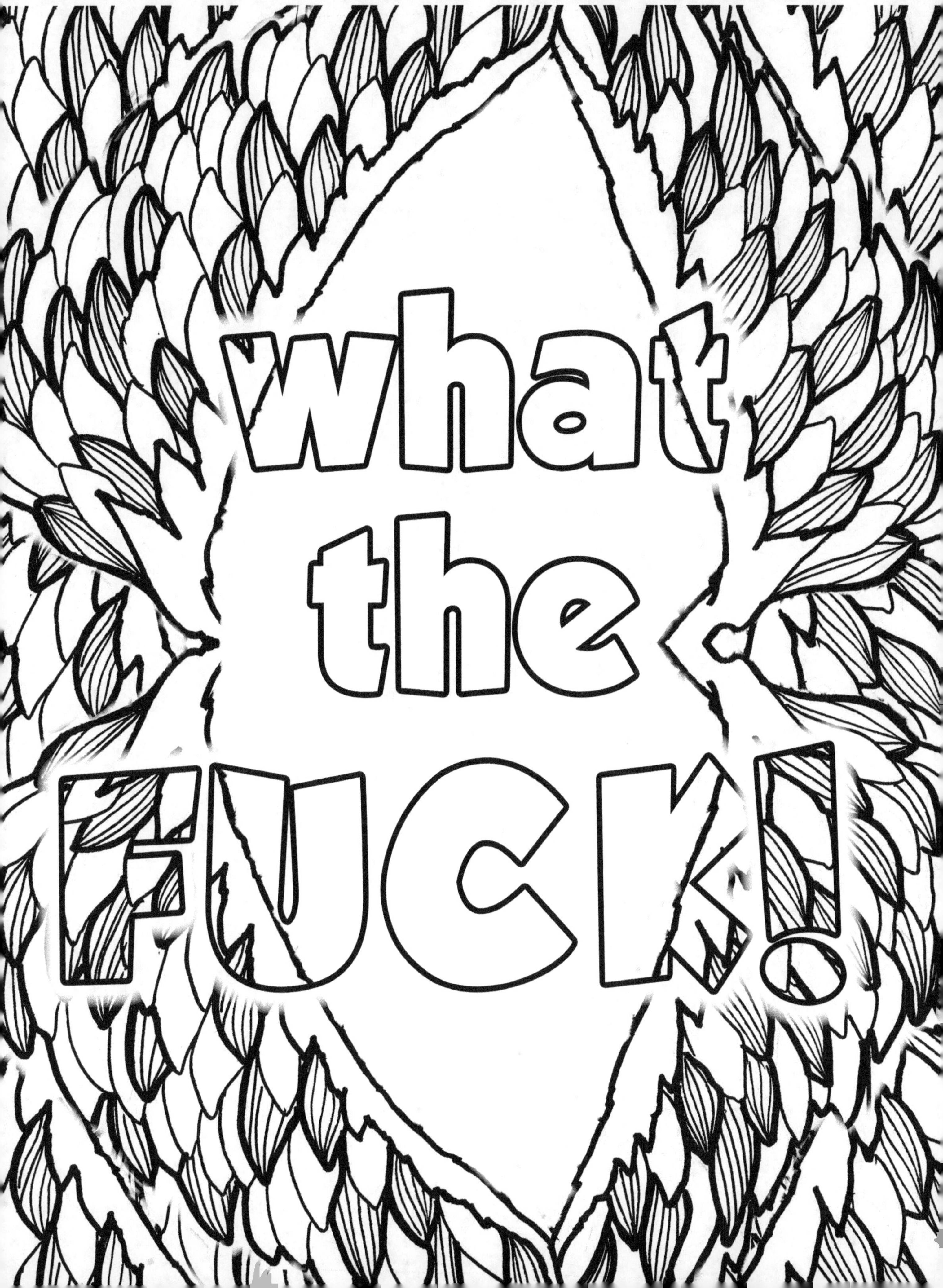
what
the
FUCK!

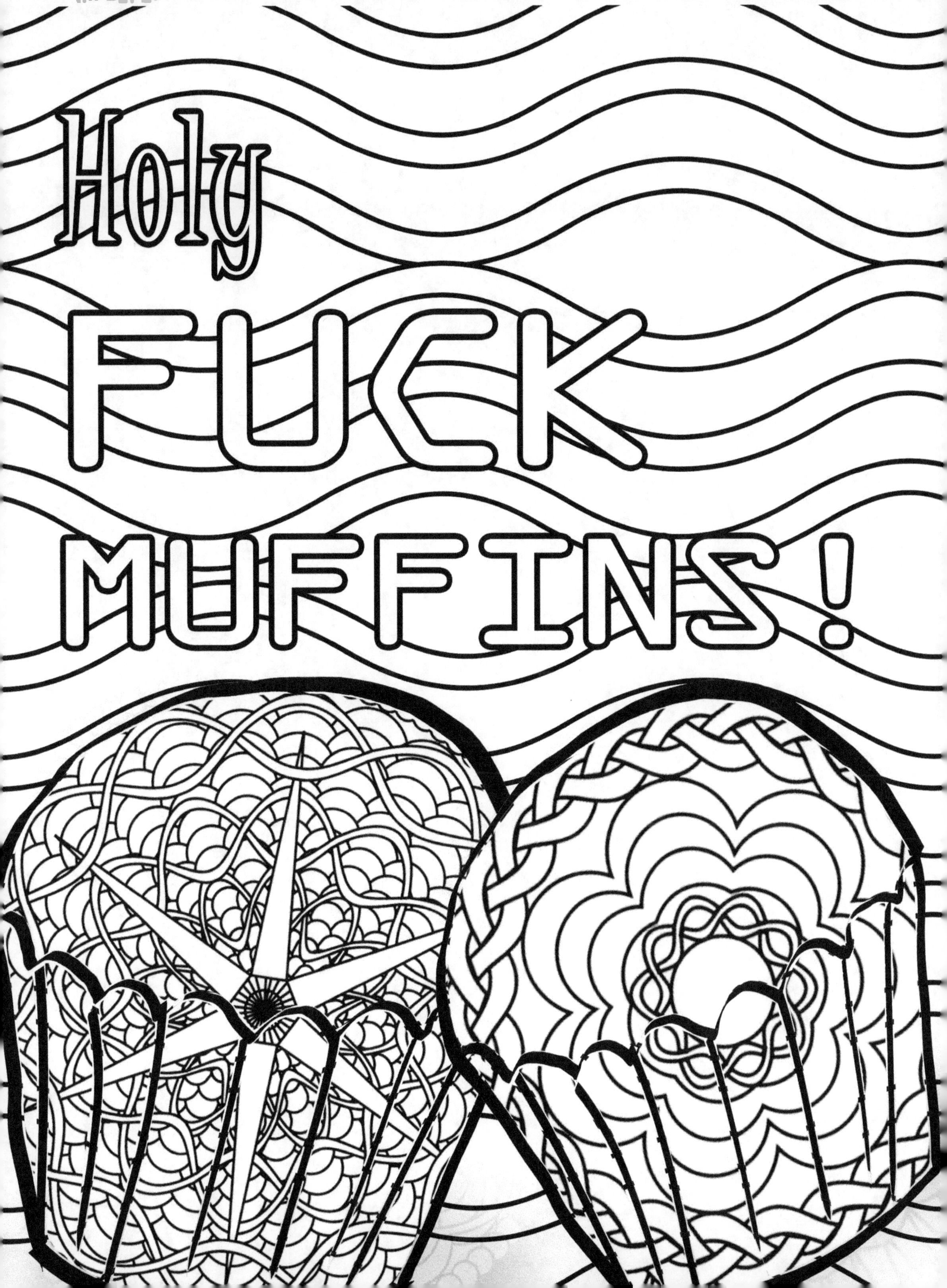
Holy
FUCK
MUFFINS!

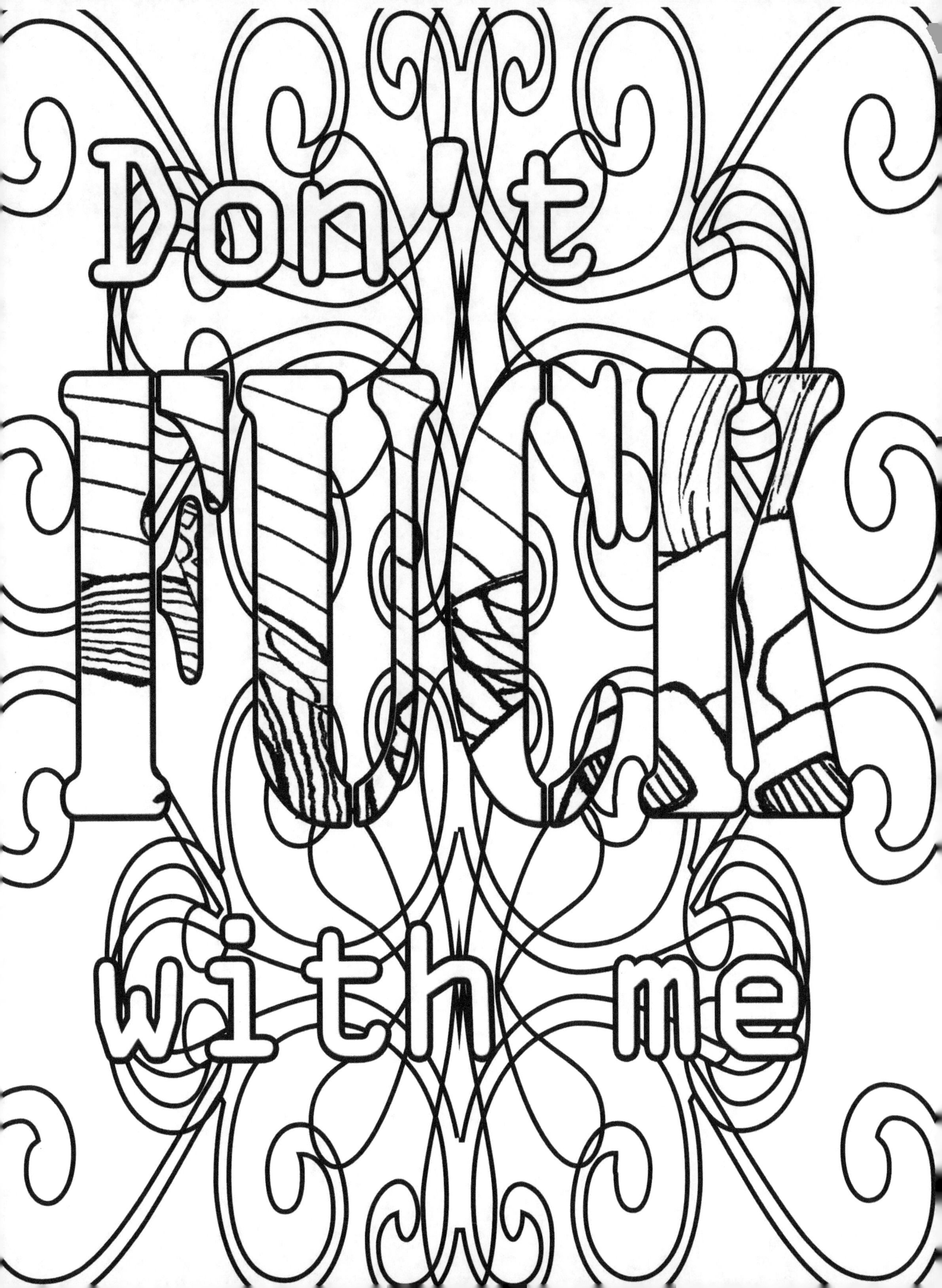
Don't
FUCK
with me

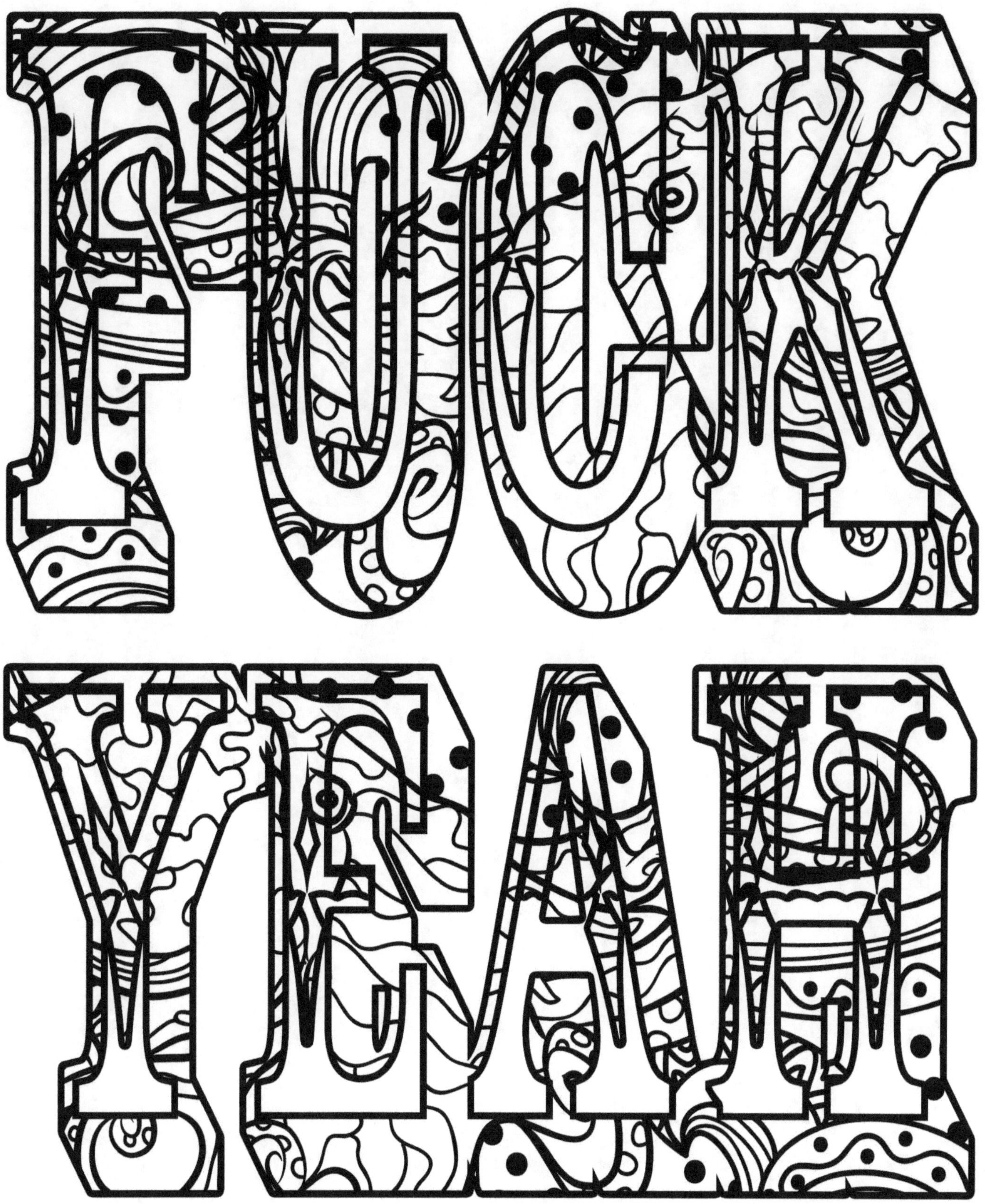
FUCK
YEAH

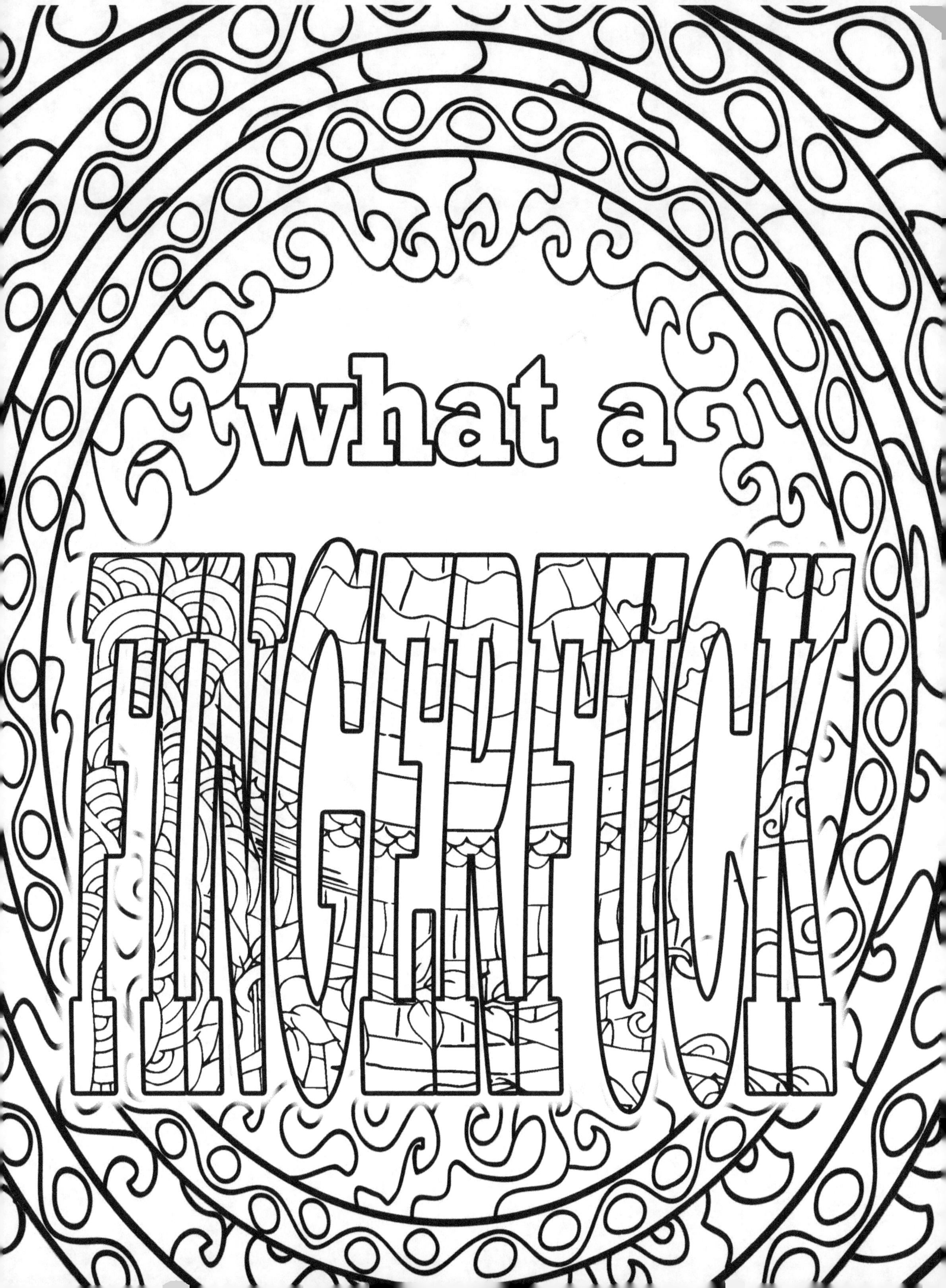
what a
FINGERFUCK

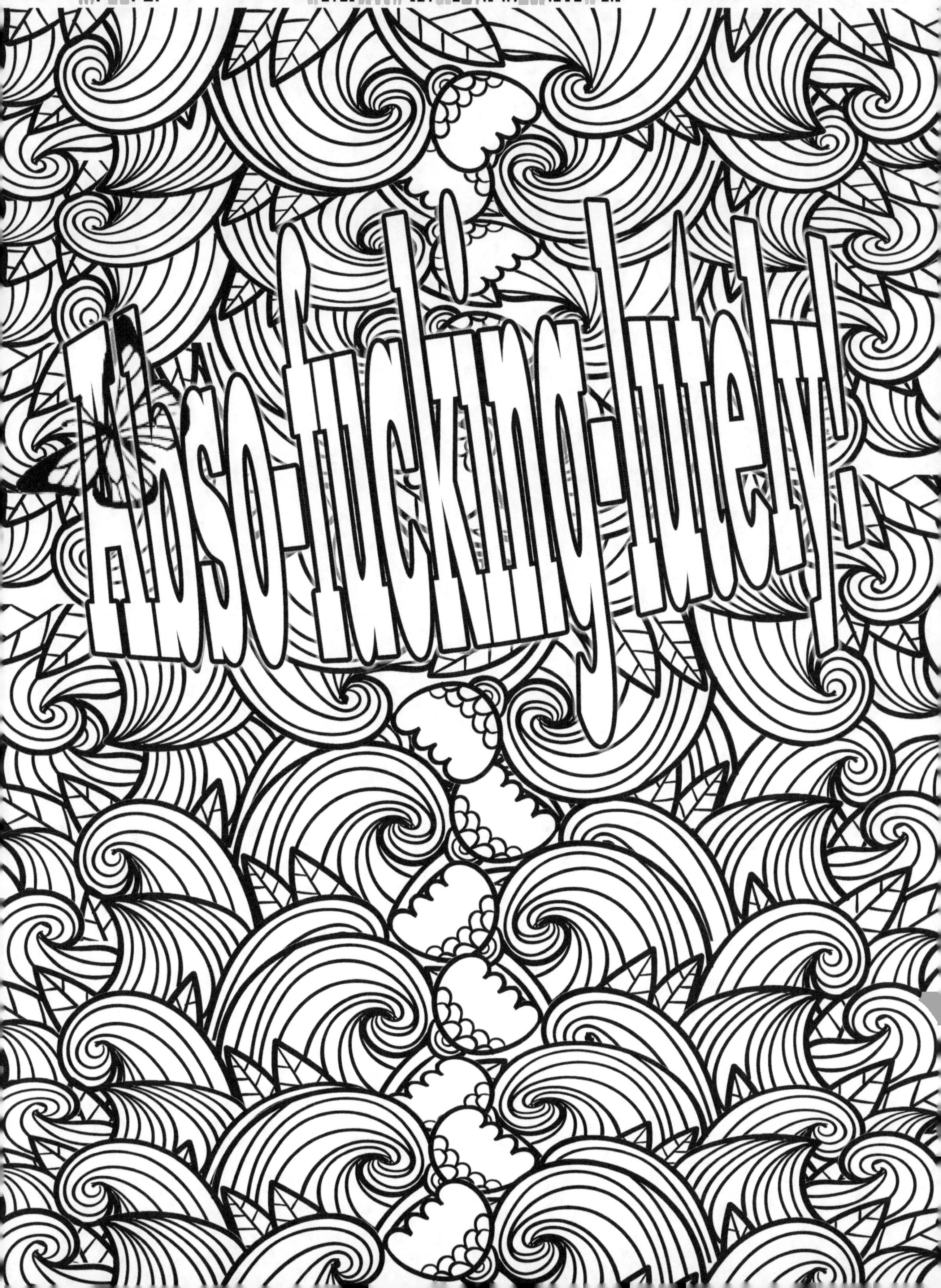
Abso-fucking-lutely!

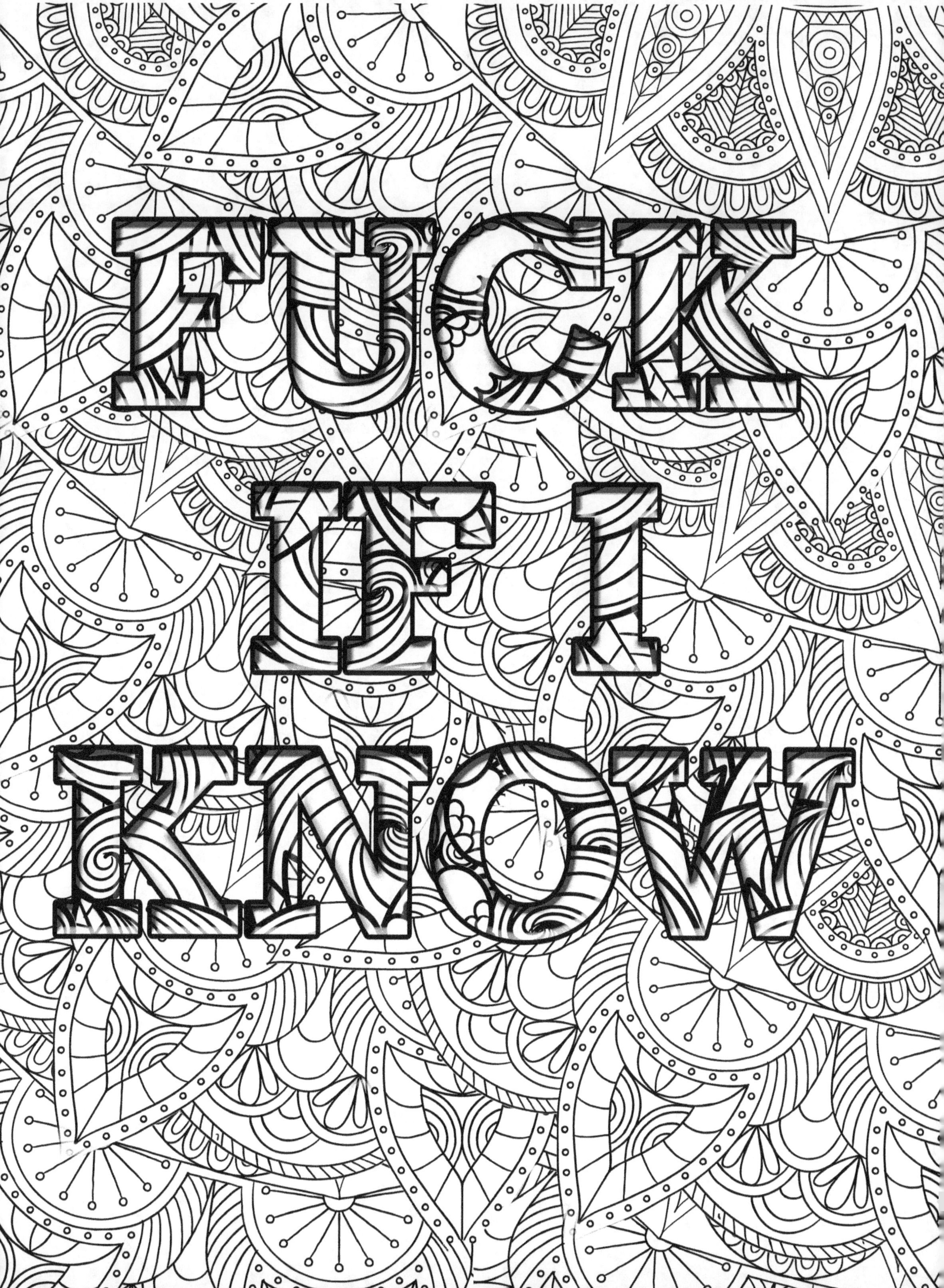
FUCK
IF I
KNOW

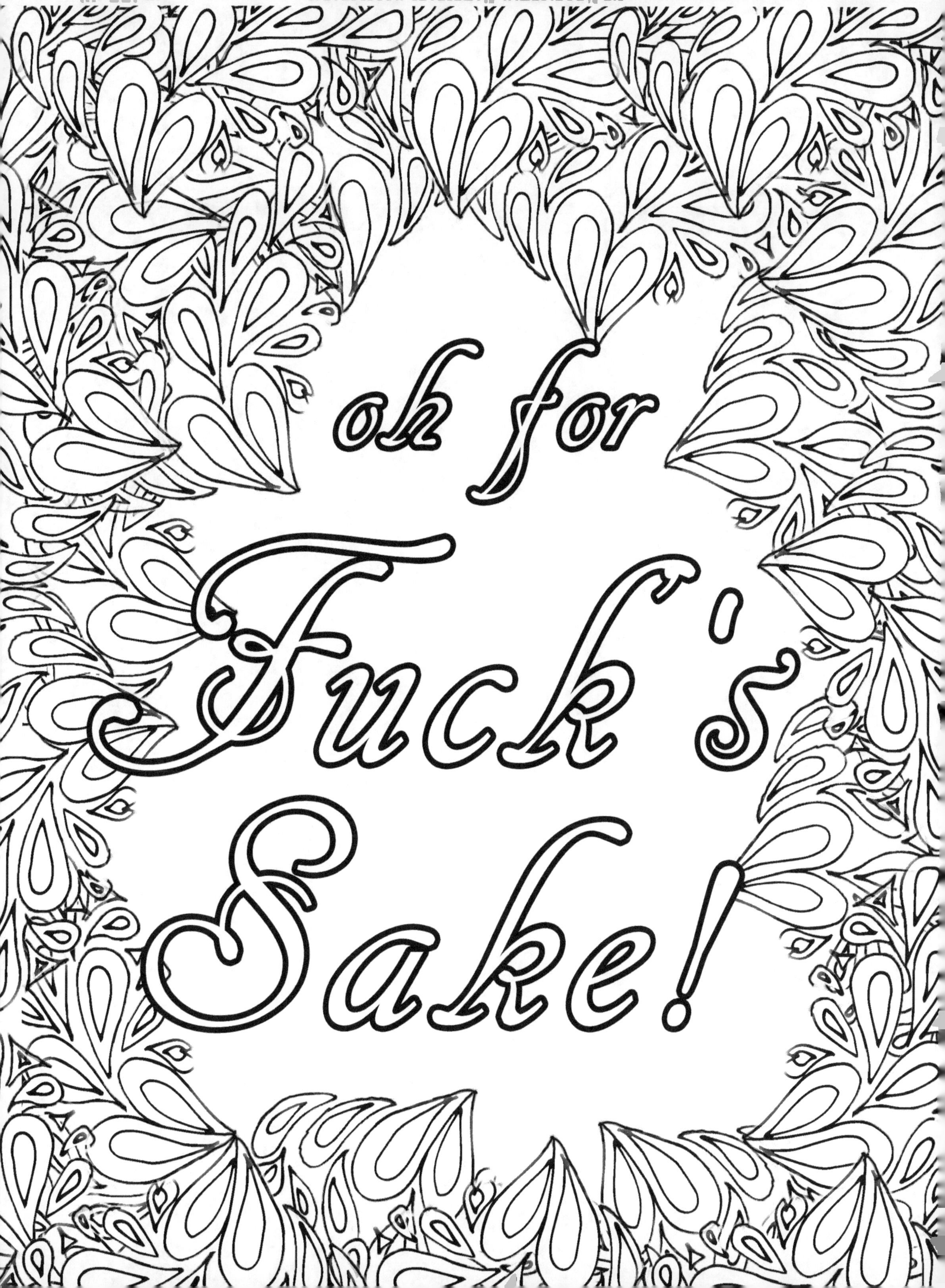
oh for
Fuck's
Sake!

More in the Adult Coloring Book series...

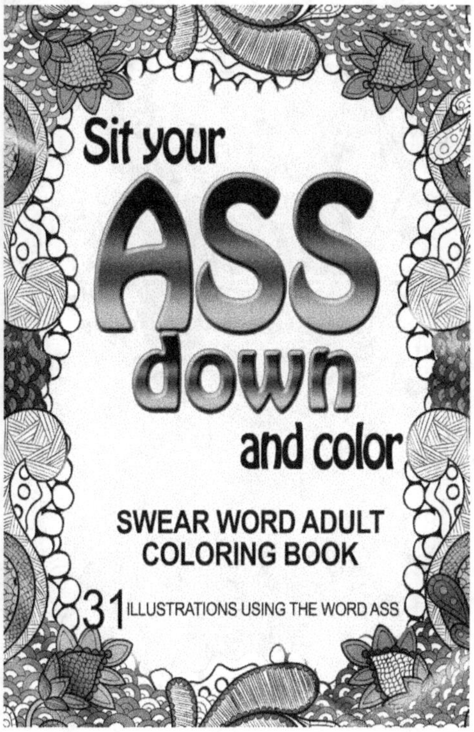

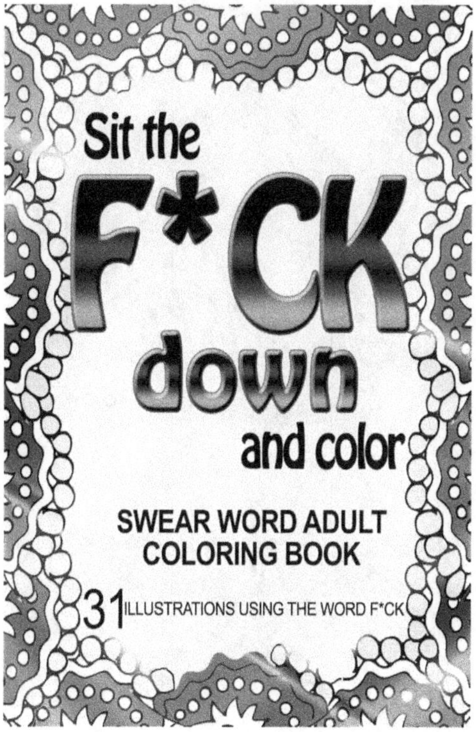

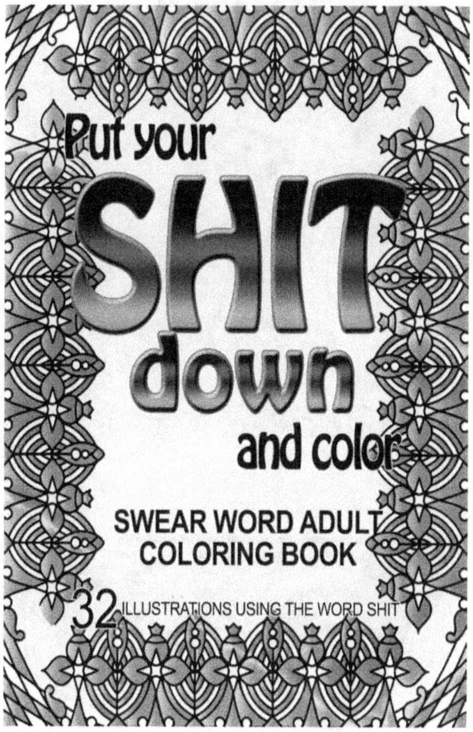

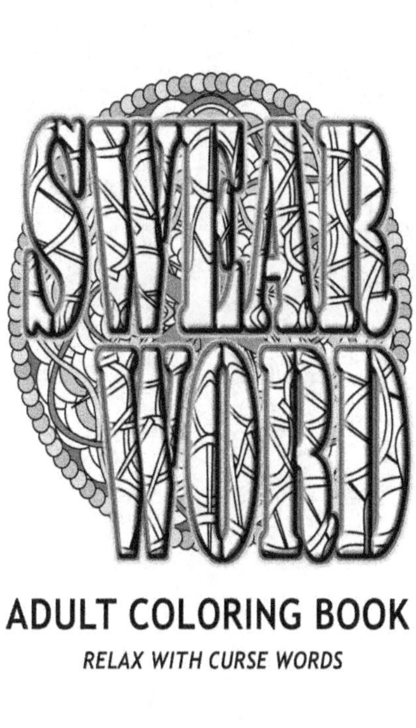

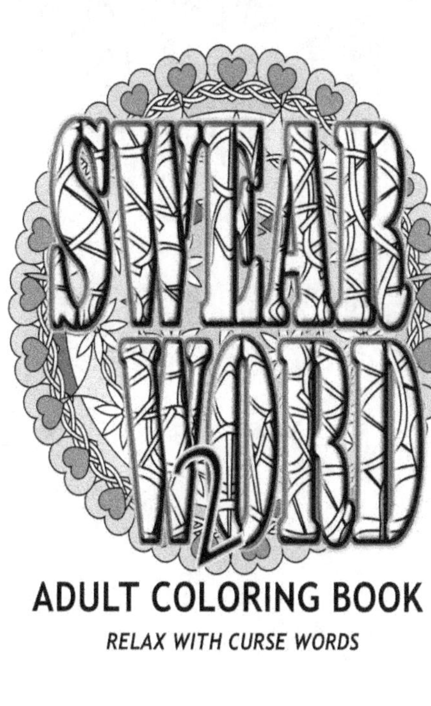

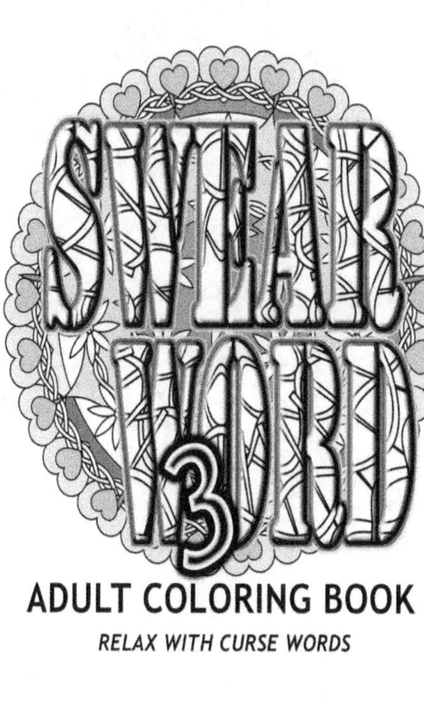

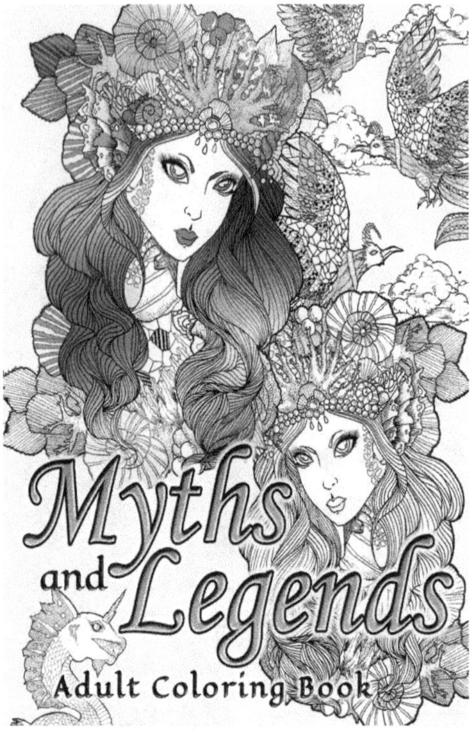
Myths and Legends
Adult Coloring Book
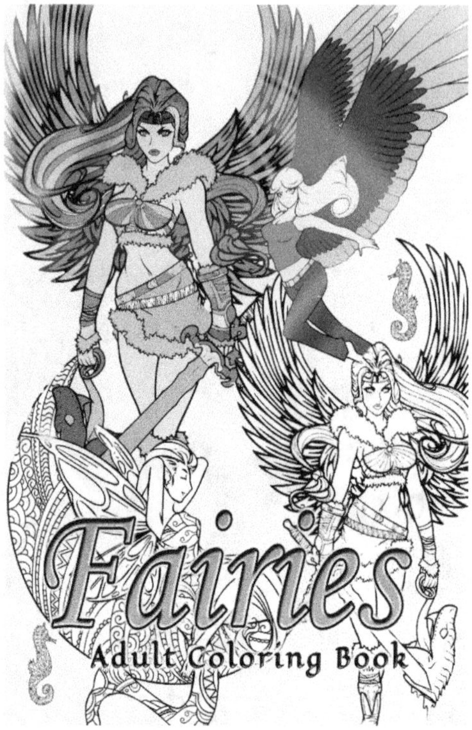
Fairies
Adult Coloring Book
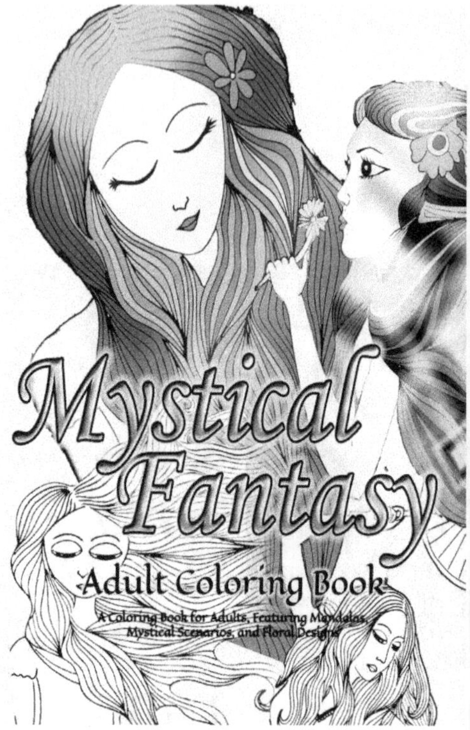
Mystical Fantasy
Adult Coloring Book
A Coloring Book for Adults, Featuring Mandalas, Mystical Scenarios, and Floral Designs
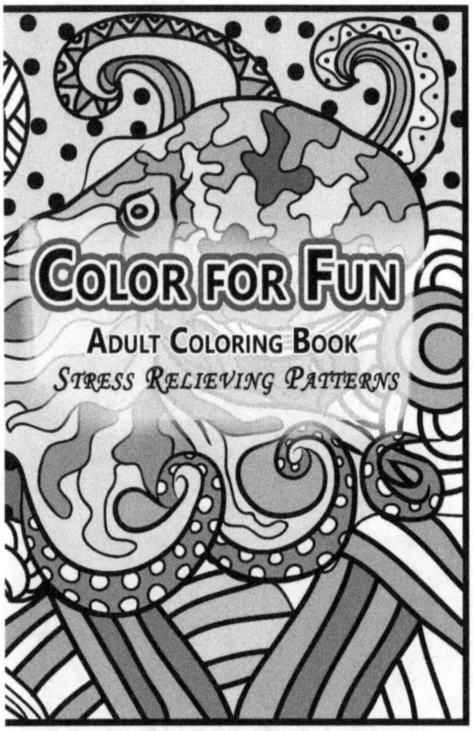
Color for Fun
Adult Coloring Book
Stress Relieving Patterns
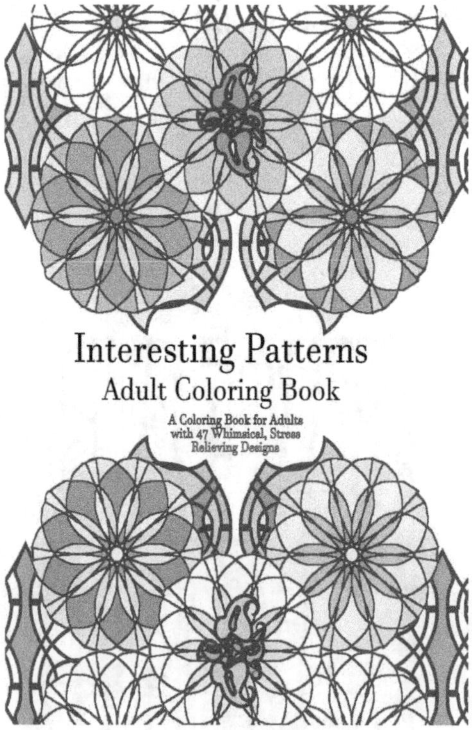
Interesting Patterns
Adult Coloring Book
A Coloring Book for Adults with 47 Whimsical, Stress Relieving Designs
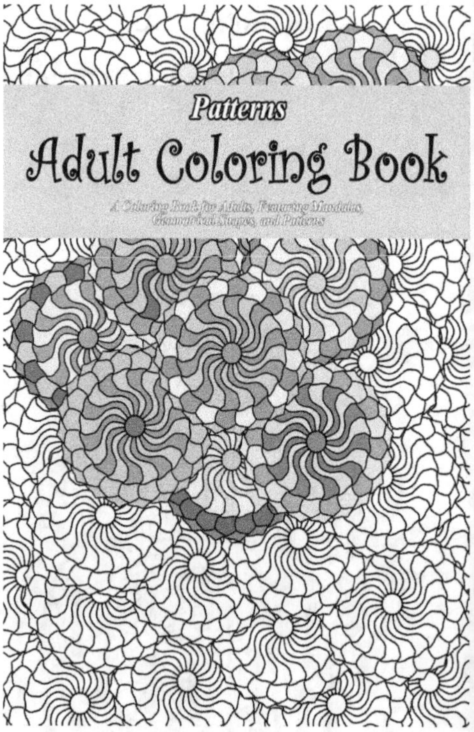
Patterns
Adult Coloring Book

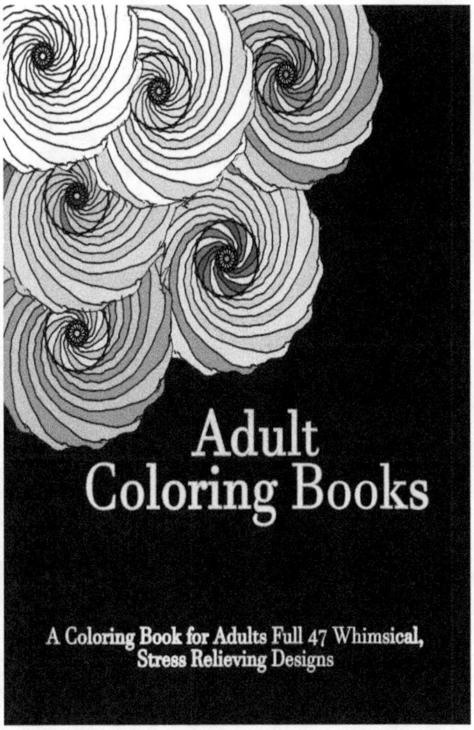
Adult
Coloring Books
A Coloring Book for Adults Full 47 Whimsical,
Stress Relieving Designs

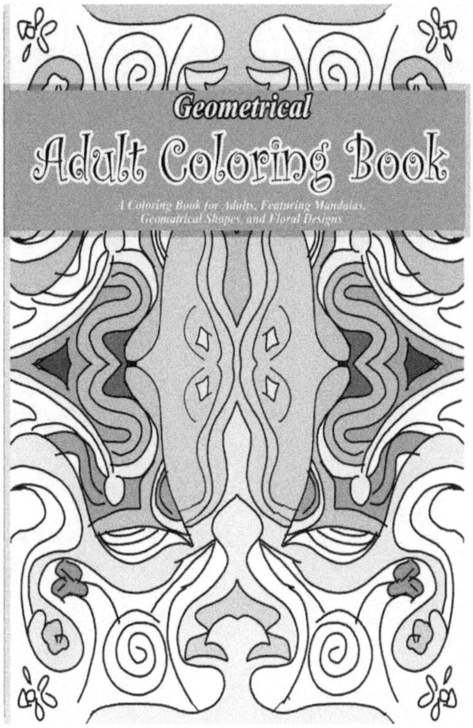
Geometrical
Adult Coloring Book
A Coloring Book for Adults, Featuring Mandalas,
Geomatrical Shapes, and Floral Designs

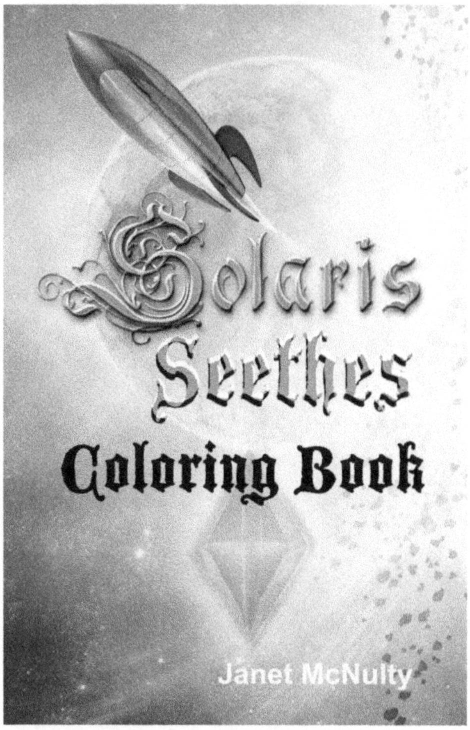
Solaris
Seethes
Coloring Book
Janet McNulty

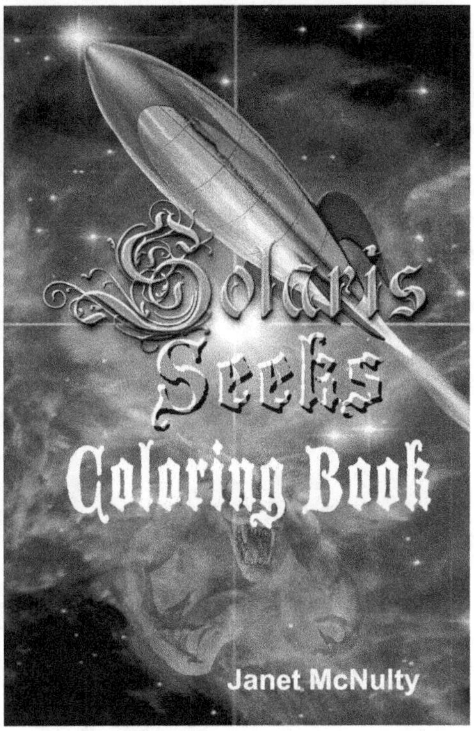
Solaris
Seeks
Coloring Book
Janet McNulty

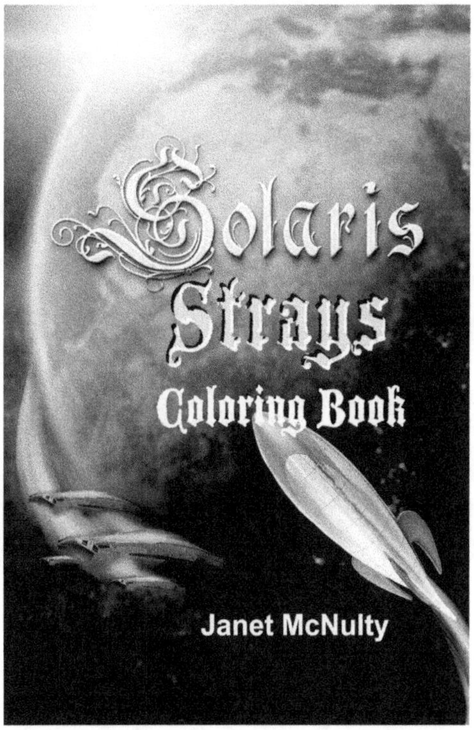
Solaris
Strays
Coloring Book
Janet McNulty

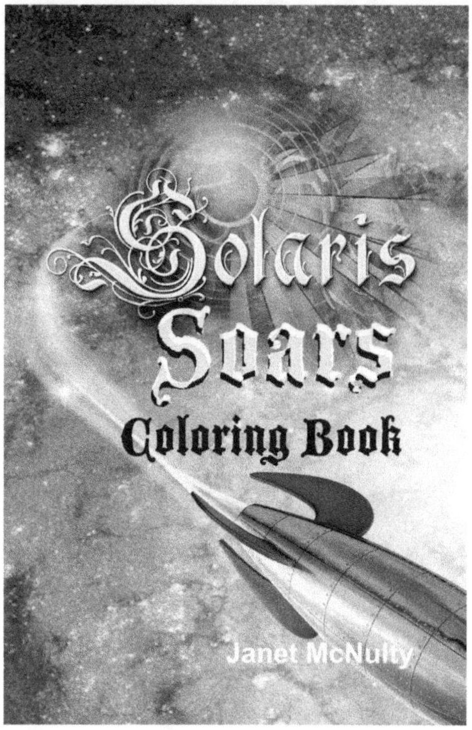
Solaris
Soars
Coloring Book
Janet McNulty

www.ingramcontent.com/pod-product-compliance
Lightning Source LLC
Chambersburg PA
CBHW080536190526
45169CB00007B/2520